The Challenge for Business and Society

The Challenge for Business and Society

From Risk to Reward

Stanley S. Litow

WILEY

Cover design: Wiley

Published by John Wiley & Sons, Inc., Hoboken, New Jersey.
Published simultaneously in Canada.

For general information on our other products and services or for technical support, please contact our Customer Care Department within the United States at (800) 762-2974, outside the United States at (317) 572-3993, or fax (317) 572-4002.

Wiley publishes in a variety of print and electronic formats and by print-on-demand. Some material included with standard print versions of this book may not be included in e-books or in print-on-demand. If this book refers to media such as a CD or DVD that is not included in the version you purchased, you may download this material at http://booksupport.wiley.com. For more information about Wiley products, visit www.wiley.com.

Library of Congress Cataloging-in-Publication Data:

Names: Litow, Stanley S., author.
Title: The challenge for business and society : from risk to reward / by
  Stanley S. Litow.
Description: Hoboken, New Jersey : John Wiley & Sons, Inc., [2018] | Includes
  index. |
Identifiers: LCCN 2018003396 (print) | LCCN 2018005296 (ebook) | ISBN
  978-1-119-437505 (epdf) | ISBN 978-1-119-43748-2 (epub) | ISBN 978-1-119-43388-0
  (cloth)
Subjects: LCSH: Social responsibility of business. | Business—Social aspects.
Classification: LCC HD60 (ebook) | LCC HD60 .L5694 2018 (print) | DDC
  658.4/08—dc23
LC record available at https://lccn.loc.gov/2018003396

Printed in the United States of America
10 9 8 7 6 5 4 3 2 1

I dedicate this book to three young people who can help us all realize a brighter future, Henry, Robinson, and Wilder, and my life partner, Amy, who makes my future brighter day by day.

Contents

Foreword

When I joined IBM in April 1993, my mandate from shareholders, the board of directors, and, yes, many employees was all about change. IBM had just reported one of the largest losses in the history of corporate America, and I was soon to learn that we were in danger of running out of cash by the end of the year. Therefore, many things had to change. We sold off underperforming businesses; we strove to reconnect with our customers; and, most urgently, we had to reduce expenses.

However, having been a great admirer of IBM during its many decades of undisputed leadership among large multinational corporations, I knew that there were pillars of strength that should be maintained and, if possible, reinforced. One of those was investments in research and development, and I made certain we protected this extraordinary resource.

Another great strength of IBM was its decades-long commitment to corporate responsibility, whether it was in civil rights, leadership in providing opportunities to women and people of color, or advances in workplace and family benefits. This, too, was an area I wanted to protect.

However, I quickly discovered that one area of corporate responsibility, namely corporate philanthropy, had, like many parts of IBM, become bogged down in bureaucracy and history. It seriously needed new leadership.

Not seeing an internal candidate, I began to search for someone to come in from outside. It didn't take long for Stan Litow to stand out as an excellent choice. He was a risk taker—a trait not found often in the philanthropic world. Moreover, he shared my personal passion for the importance of reforming K–12 education in America. I had worked for more than 30 years prior to coming to IBM on many efforts aimed at trying to fix our public schools, and I knew I wanted the new IBM to throw its many resources behind this important effort.

Stan turned out to be everything I needed to reinvigorate IBM's long-standing commitment to public service. For a decade, we worked side by side on a very active corporate responsibility agenda. And much of it focused on K–12 reform.

Stan then supported my successor, Sam Palmisano, for another decade as IBM further expanded its philanthropic work. Finally, the indefatigable man, Stan went on to serve so well Sam's successor, Ginni Rometty.

This book discusses many of the activities that Stan led so successfully at IBM. This focus is understandable since he had a distinguished 25-year career at the company. However, Stan also draws on many examples from other companies, and as a result this book should be helpful to all those businessmen and -women who believe strongly in the importance of corporate philanthropy.

On a personal note, I am unabashedly a proponent of active corporate citizenship. I know there are some in the business community who do not share this view. When our communities are healthy and, hopefully, thriving, the companies in these communities enjoy many levels of support. Conversely, operating a business in a declining, negative environment only adds to the challenge of corporate leadership. Effective public-private partnerships almost always benefit both participants.

The business community is under considerable pressure today. Whether it is income inequity, jobs lost to Asia or Mexico, stagnant wages, or tax avoidance, citizens as well as politicians are pointing fingers at the business community. Responding to these criticisms will require far more than good corporate citizenship. Nevertheless, greater attention to all the ways businesses can support our communities will be a very important ingredient in any significant repositioning of American business in the eyes of America's politicians, media, and academics, as well as its employees and ordinary citizens.

Lou Gerstner
December 14, 2017

Acknowledgments

The content of this book draws heavily on my professional experience in the public sector, private sector, and civil society. I have been fortunate to have had substantial experience in all three sectors over a long period of time. My colleagues in all my work experiences have been extremely valuable as colleagues and as friends. Working in the administration of John V. Lindsay during his tenure as mayor of New York City offered me a unique leadership opportunity at an early age on issues facing the city. My associates at the Urban Corps under the leadership of Deputy Mayor Tim Costello helped me to learn and grow as a professional and create a meaningful range of opportunities for college students to contribute to the functioning of the city, benefiting all city residents.

In the creation and operation of Interface and the Educational Priorities Panel, both of which I led, I had a unique opportunity to develop policy studies and advocacy strategies that assisted the city as it coped with and then recovered from a massive financial crisis. I had a good deal of help in that effort from many colleagues. In my tenure as deputy schools chancellor I had an opportunity to work with one of America's finest education leaders, Joseph Fernandez, and adept political leaders like Bobby Wagner and Carl McCall, as well as many colleagues in my IBM tenure under three CEOs—Lou Gerstner, who hired me, and Sam Palmisano and Ginni Rometty, who succeeded him—I benefited from their strong leadership and consistent support.

The colleagues who worked with me and supported me throughout my career in government, the private sector, and civil society are far too many to mention, but I'd like to call out the following: David Lebenstein, Jill Blair, John Mattoon, Tina Kelly, Ariel Zwang, Jim Vlasto, Kim Bohen, Sarah Williams, Jen Crozier, Gina Tesla, Doris Gonzalez, Grace Suh, Maura Banta, Diane Melley, Ann Cramer, John Tolva, Sherry Swick, Donna Mattoon, Rashid Davis, Kevin Rothman, Karen Amaker, Armando Rodriguez, and so many more. Julius Edelstein and Al Bowker, both now deceased, were very valuable mentors and dear friends.

Apart from my professional experiences, I have benefited from close friends and family who have supported me in everything I have been able to accomplish, especially my son and daughter, Andrew and Alexandra, their spouses, Lauryn and Ryan, and my especially my life partner, Amy Brenna, who has been there for me every step of the way.

Introduction

For those who knew me well at the beginning of my career, my writing a book about corporations and their role in society would really be odd. I began my professional career in the mayor's office in New York City, and after four years of helping shape city policy and managing the largest public-service internship program in the country, I founded and led a not-for-profit think tank and community advocacy organization. Following that I served as deputy schools chancellor, helping lead the nation's largest school district through a period of turbulence. My experience in city government, education, and not-for-profit enterprise expanded my views on public policy and provided knowledge on issues like education, but a deep knowledge of corporations was not among my assets. I basically saw the private sector as just another funder for my reform ideas. I lacked substantive knowledge about the private sector. Of course, that all changed when Lou Gerstner, then IBM's CEO, while leading a massive corporate turnaround, recruited me to IBM to lead corporate citizenship. In over two decades, and under the leadership of three IBM CEOs, I've gained intimate knowledge of the private sector and specifically its role in society. That is why the most recent U.S. presidential election sparked my interest in writing this book.

The 2016 presidential campaign focused a good deal of attention—overwhelmingly negative—on the role of corporations in society. Big companies were accused of a range of sins—profiteering, plundering the environment, ignoring (even exacerbating) societal ills ranging from illiteracy and discrimination to obesity and opioid addiction. Income inequality, a particularly contentious and divisive issue, was laid squarely at the doorstep of billionaires and the private sector. Wall Street, in particular, was a convenient target for the blame for growth in income inequality, by contrasting the lack of growth in wages with the growing number of billionaires.

But the angry rhetoric hardly stopped at Wall Street, and wasn't restricted only to financial services. Quite the contrary: companies with manufacturing plants outside the United States were criticized for sending jobs abroad, companies that cut jobs in the United States, even in the face of declining revenue, those that embraced or created technology that could eliminate jobs. In fact, while some of the criticism was justified, nearly all companies were vilified regardless of whether their behavior justified it.

At the same time, there is another side. President Donald Trump, who joined in a good deal of the criticism of the private sector during the campaign, shifted. He moved federal policy and rhetoric in a totally different direction. He got rid of fiscal, social, and environmental rules that purportedly hobbled business, reduced or shut down cabinet offices historically protecting the public good, and rolled back clean power, consumer protection, civil rights, and living wage and healthy eating initiatives, and he endorsed moving basic public funding from public to private schools—all in the spirit of addressing the need for private-sector job growth and a reduced public-sector role. The privatization of public services seems to have gained renewed interest from some in government, including expanding the privatization of the military. While some view this positively, it may have another effect, exacerbating the negative views held by increasing numbers of Americans who see corporations, especially large corporations, in a decidedly bad light.

To many, this ushers in a new era of "cowboy capitalism." Big companies, unfettered by regulation, encouraged by the presidential bully pulpit, are freed up to go about the business of making money—no matter the consequences to consumers and the commonweal. If there is little or no growth in wages, especially among those on the wrong end of the income inequality spectrum, we can expect the negative rhetoric,

I have learned from my leadership roles in the public, nonprofit, and private sectors, as well as from working with U.S. presidents, governors, mayors, CEOs, and nonprofit leaders, that the most successful companies prosper by actively choosing to produce positive change. Those that do not—and there are far too many of them—will face significant long-term downsides.

When I served as New York City's deputy schools chancellor in the early 1990s during a serious economic downturn, with the city budget in free fall, the budget of America's largest school system was in serious jeopardy and the City of New York faced the possibility of having its bonds downgraded. Draconian cuts were in the offing, motivated by the need for budget cuts and reallocations, but also to demonstrate to the rating agencies that the city was serious about managing its way through this difficult economic downturn.

The school system needed innovative solutions. Among the solutions I came up with, two are worth reviewing. One involved a negotiation with the city's powerful teachers' union to cluster agreed-upon vacation days into the week of Lincoln's and Washington's birthdays to provide school system employees with a no-cost-added week of vacation. What became known as the midwinter recess was offered to teachers in return for over $200 million in financial concessions that would close a significant budget shortfall. It worked. But to build public support required all sectors to step up and support the change. The business community provided significant leadership on this issue via the Partnership for New York City and with individual business leaders going out front in support of the plan.

A second idea, also impacting the teachers' unions, was to negotiate an early retirement program. It entailed costs that would be shared with the city and the school system, but it also had potential savings in the short and especially the long term. This too involved winning over business support. Again, the Partnership and individual CEOs like Fred Salerno, who worked for the predecessor of Verizon, spoke out publicly and visited the mayor, comptroller, and members of the city council to voice their support. In both instances, as I sought their help, I learned about the significant influence that business could have on political and governmental decision making.

coupled with demonstrations and community actions, to escalate history tells us anything, this new era will stimulate a counterreacti at the state and local levels. This would certainly not be the first time period of corporate ambition led to a negative reaction. In the 1920 corporate behavior led to the worst financial crisis America had eve seen, with the Great Depression, resulting in the onset of the New Deal in the 1930s, which increased governmental authority over business. In fact, America's views about corporations wax and wane. Efforts to over-regulate in the 1970s led to the election of Ronald Reagan and a very different set of actions during the 1980s.

Where are we today? Frankly, it seems like a train wreck waiting to happen. But we do have a choice. We always do. We can simply sit back and let it all unfold before our eyes, or instead, beginning with a fact-based assessment of history and reality, we can actively participate in efforts to balance the growth of business with the needs of society to produce genuine shared benefit.

Some corporations, freed from regulations, will abuse the public trust. Others will respond effectively in their communities and with their employees, investing more, not less, in social and environmental areas, working hand in hand with local and state governments and non-profits to address societal challenges, especially the critical issues of education and job creation. How many will act this way and how they do it will be the major issue—whether there are one-shot efforts to counter bad behavior by others, or instead systemic solutions; whether they are scalable, sustainable, and a model for others. While President Trump has promised to reduce "foreign aid," some big companies might actually do the opposite, and step up efforts to engage with communities around the world, not just in the United States, assisting in job creation, poverty alleviation, and improvements in education and health.

Some might choose to address the growing jobs and skills crises. They may do this for a range of reasons, such as to impact their bottom line, advantage civil society, engage employees, and reflect positively with their shareholders. But the motivation for this action will be critically important. Some will see it as in their business interest to focus on actions designed to impact favorably on society. Others will see it as core to their corporate culture, values, and beliefs, understanding its value in attracting and retaining top young talent. Some will combine both, and hopefully influence others.

The two efforts I outlined were implemented, saved hundreds of millions of dollars, and avoided both teacher layoffs and classroom service reductions. Several years later I championed a plan to get the schools recognized as a licensed Medicare provider and therefore be eligible to obtain hundreds of millions of dollars in federal reimbursements for needed and necessary services. And once again my supporters in the business community were there, advocating in Albany, Washington, and City Hall. Their support was critical. While I learned a good deal about the influence of business and its leaders on vital city services, I knew little about its basic operations or its strategy.

Much has been written about successful corporate strategies in finance and marketing, advertising and research, and too little about corporate behavior at the nexus of business and society. There are in fact clear benefits.

First and foremost, positive actions affecting society assist in recruiting and retaining top talent. This is perhaps the most important competitive advantage sought by companies. And it is clear that responsible business behavior gives companies access to top talent, and is oftentimes as effective as increasing salaries or expanding employee benefits. In one frequently cited example, there are more students in the social enterprise club at the Harvard Business School than in all the other clubs on campus combined. Study after study verifies that young prospective employees will screen out employment opportunities offered by companies that are not effective corporate citizens.

Second, good corporate behavior will build support in communities and within government, providing assets that companies need to avoid risk. In fact, many governmental requests for proposals (RFPs) for business opportunities now require bidders to outline the benefits they provide to their communities.

Third, it will stimulate community support, among existing or prospective clients and other stakeholders, and assist in establishing new markets. Some companies require their vendors to release corporate responsibility reports, while others insist on outside independent audits of such behavior. For publicly traded companies, this engenders the support of shareholders and a positive response from socially responsible investors who control trillions of dollars in assets. There was a time when such investors simply declined to invest in companies that produced questionable products such as alcohol and tobacco. But the current practice goes far beyond that to examine broader business behavior. In short, executed effectively, corporate responsibility limits risk and maximizes reward for companies, producing a return on investment.

Beauty Is in the Eye of the Beholder

When it comes to the role of the private sector, the phrase "beauty is in the eye of the beholder" truly fits. However, it is important to go beyond opinion and stereotypes and look at the facts. There are many examples of private-sector job growth and economic progress across the United States and globally as a result of strong and responsible corporate leadership.

Yet there are also plenty of examples of horrific bad behavior on the part of the private sector. (The same is true, by the way, when we look at government and civil society.) At this juncture, it is important to thoughtfully examine what leads to both positive and negative conduct, detail how businesses can move forward in the most productive way possible, and determine what specifically would result were we to do more than just encourage higher levels of performance, or fine or lock up those who abuse the public trust. America has always seen its future deeply connected to the development and growth of the private sector. Industrial growth in the United States fueled an economic engine that flourished in the latter half of the nineteenth century and was sustained well into the twentieth. It allowed the country to assume global leadership, and provided opportunities for a growing middle class. It fulfilled the promise of the American dream for many working-class and immigrant Americans. Clearly, the free enterprise system has had some negatives, and it is important to understand what they are, but overall, America's private-sector growth and development is a decidedly positive story, deeply connected to American values.

Motivation for companies to serve the common good extends beyond philanthropy or the virtue of individual leaders. Top companies that engage in positive behavior, use that behavior to attract and keep the best employees, generate esprit de corps, produce superior products and services, and appeal to consumers by responding positively to societal challenges. Specific examples tell the story. Paid vacations began in the private sector, as did paid sick and maternity leave. They were not legislated, regulated, or mandated by government. They had a cost, but in the view of those who pioneered them, the benefit exceeded the cost, especially over the long term. The same is true of employer health care and retirement benefits. Both had benefits that were greater than the costs. More recently, this proactive leadership has included recognition of same-sex marriage, child and senior care, and other employer-supported services.

Past Is Prologue: The History of Corporate Responsibility

Corporate philanthropy in the United States started as an outgrowth not of business practices, but of personal philanthropy practiced by some of the nineteenth century's iconic American business figures. Andrew Carnegie, John D. Rockefeller, Henry Ford, and J. P. Morgan were major business leaders whose business careers brought them great wealth and power. During their careers, they were often ruthless in their quest for money. Anything that stood in their way was fair game. Their outsized wealth and questionable business practices often made them a target for scorn. However, at the end of their careers, many began personal philanthropic activities. The philanthropies they set up and endowed live on today. Carnegie's funds began the public library systems. Rockefeller championed health care and education. The Ford, Rockefeller, Carnegie, and Mellon Foundations survive a hundred years past their donors' deaths, affecting how people view the individuals whose wealth endowed these charities and foundations, and it is likely that the institutions enabled by their wealth will continue into the foreseeable future. But personal philanthropy had little to do with their corporate behavior, corporate responsibility, or business practices. The companies that these iconic philanthropists led were often examples not of the best but of the worst corporate behavior toward their employees, communities, and society. Rarely, if ever, did these individual philanthropists couple personal generosity with their core business practices.

When we examine labor practices, there are myriad examples of extremely bad behavior. A seven-day workweek that disabled workers and cut their lives short; a twelve- to fourteen-hour workdays and abusive child labor practices that also ended lives; low wages; unsafe work environments; and discrimination on the basis of race, gender, and ethnicity all promulgated by the private sector sustained poverty, destabilized communities, and led to serious distress. This is part of our nation's history.

We can't hide from this history. And here again, I have a personal connection to such corporate behavior, and in this case, it is far from positive. I had a grandmother who entered the United States as an immigrant from Russia at the turn of the twentieth century. As with so many Jewish immigrants who came to New York City, she settled on Manhattan's Lower East Side and went to work at the Triangle Shirtwaist Factory. The factory eventually burned, killing many of its workers. Luckily for my grandmother, this fire happened after she left, but the disaster resulted from a workspace that was unsafe, with horrendous working conditions. Triangle's leadership paid a price, but the workers paid a much heavier one.

At the same time these terrible practices were taking place, there were examples of positive leadership. Most people might think that paid vacations or sick leave were pioneered by government and launched via governmental law or regulation. The reverse is true. In the early part of the twentieth century, in 1902, National Cash Register via the leadership of its founder and CEO, John Patterson, began offering employees a full week of unpaid vacation. Shortly thereafter, this was converted to paid vacation. At that time neither the federal government nor any state offered its employees vacations, paid or unpaid. The rationale, according to another CEO of the era, Walter Camp, who also implemented paid vacation, was to stimulate "loyalty and good performance." Interestingly, at that time, while government lagged behind the private sector in this labor practice, President William Howard Taft, a Republican often thought of as a fiscal and social conservative, spoke out positively about the notion of paid vacations, though he never turned his ideas into legislative or policy proposals. In the 1910s, a survey of 163 large companies across the United States found that 43 had paid vacation policies.

Since that time, companies have expanded paid vacation policies to include a number of other noteworthy practices, including sick leave, health insurance, child care, domestic partner benefits, paid family leave, family benefits, and policies against discrimination. Sometimes these policies were stimulated by advocacy and championed by government leaders or labor unions, but just as frequently they were instituted by the companies themselves to instill loyalty, improve productivity, aid recruitment or retention, and especially to maintain a competitive advantage. The impetus was to encourage productivity and higher levels of performance.

The history of private pension plans is equally important. The private sector, not government, led by what is now the American Express Company, which was reinventing itself and its business model, created a private pension plan, half a century before any government in the nation did at either the local, state, or federal level. They were pathbreakers. Employer-provided health insurance also has a long history predating government. Some large companies instituted such policies in the early part of the twentieth century, though when employers were accorded tax benefits at the end of the Second World War, such benefits expanded, with large companies like AT&T, General Motors, U.S. Steel, and others providing significant health benefits. Oftentimes the benefits gave companies a competitive advantage, much in the way pension benefits did, and positively affected employees. Also at the end of the Second World War, some companies began to pioneer providing maternity benefits.

More recently, companies enacted family leave policies, same-sex partner benefits, and early childhood and elder care. Companies like Starbucks proudly put in place large-scale higher education tuition benefits. Others provide incentives to employees who use solar heating in their homes and/or provide financial benefit to employees who purchase or lease hybrid or electric vehicles. None of these practices were regulated or legislated. They largely have been designed and delivered to respond to the interest and motivation of the workforce and were intended to attract and retain workers and make them more productive. A review of such practices makes it clear that they predate interest from government and any effort to legislate or regulate such practices. But they have not been embraced by all employers, with far too many lagging behind.

In the 1930s, President Franklin D. Roosevelt and his secretary of labor, Frances Perkins—the first woman to serve in a president's cabinet—led an effort to enact Social Security, perhaps the most fundamental reform ever to take place in U.S. government history. While the Affordable Care Act, or Obamacare, is a critical twenty-first-century effort, Social Security improved income equality and economic security for all in retirement. To turn this new, forward-looking law from concept into reality, the president and his secretary of labor reached out to IBM CEO Tom Watson, whose innovative technology and public-spirited activities enabled this reform to be implemented. In many ways, it was a prototype of today's popular public-private partnership. While referenced from time to time, the full story of the creation and growth of Social Security has never been fully told. It involved the application of technology, to be sure, but it also involved a deep public-private partnership built around issues of trust and personal responsibility. Social Security benefited the United States and its government, assisted in the exit from the Great Depression, and also led to IBM's growth and the growth of the tech industry.

Watson's son, Thomas Watson Jr., was a leader in the civil rights movement, but for a number of practical business reasons, in the 1950s he focused on Lexington, Kentucky, as the location for a new manufacturing plant to turn out printers, and yet were IBM to open its plant in Lexington it would have to be segregated to conform to standard southern practice. In negotiations with the then governor of Kentucky, Watson made it clear that if the plant were to open in Lexington it would have to be integrated. The governor pushed back, but ultimately relented. IBM's Lexmark plant was fully integrated when it opened, and that led to the integration of the schools in Lexington as well. IBM under Watson's leadership also opened a plant in Raleigh, North Carolina, in what became Research Triangle Park, or RTP. Although it didn't happen overnight, locating IBM's plants in Kentucky and North Carolina ultimately helped fuel economic growth in the South and bolstered the case for ending segregation.

In the 1990s, IBM continued its corporate transformation, moving from old-style technologies onto the cusp of the twenty-first century with new and innovative technologies that fueled tech's resurgence. This happened during the tenure of a transformational CEO, Lou Gerstner, who rescued the company from near bankruptcy. In the late 1980s, under Presidents Ronald Reagan and George H. W. Bush, a spotlight was focused on the failures of the American education system. That spotlight continued to shine brightly into the early to mid-1990s under President Bill Clinton. But by the middle of the 1990s, efforts at school reform were stalled. Corporate leaders spoke out and responded to presidential leadership, participating in meetings and discussions at the state and local levels and responding positively to calls to "Join a School" and "Adopt a School." But while well intentioned, most of these efforts were reactive and neither structural nor transformative. Evaluations of such efforts conducted by the Harvard Business School revealed them to be more than disappointing. And by the early 1990s they had lost their momentum.

In 1995, Gerstner delivered the keynote address at a National Governors Association gathering, calling for more ambitious reform. He told the governors that they were the CEOs of their states, and as CEOs, they had responsibility for the quality of their schools. His leadership led to three National Education Summits, all held not at the White House, but at IBM's Learning Center, led by a group of CEOs and governors. Gerstner handpicked CEOs from other large companies like Boeing, AT&T, and State Farm to join him as conveners. These summits under IBM's and Gerstner's leadership created a consensus behind the need for standards and accountability. Republican governors like Tommy Thompson of Wisconsin and John Engler of Michigan, leaders in their states for educational reform, and Democratic governors like Jim Hunt of North Carolina and Roy Romer of Colorado, also leaders within their party, were equally engaged. A new nonprofit called Achieve was created to implement the plan that emerged from the summit. This story, which is deeply connected to America's controversy over the Common Core curriculum, received front-page treatment at the time, and while reported on sporadically, it has never fully been told. It is a vitally important story with lessons for the future. I had the opportunity to manage some of these activities during the 1996, 1999, and 2001 summits and participated firsthand in the collaborative work between CEOs and governors that resulted.

Where We Are Today

Since IBM is the company I know best, I will start there, though there are many examples of leadership by others. As IBM moved into the twenty-first century, corporate responsibility continued its transformation with extensive investments balancing business strategy and social good, producing significant results.

The creation of new technologies like grid computing was the foundation for the building of a free virtual supercomputer called World Community Grid, harnessing the computing power of nearly one million computing devices around the world. Today it supports hundreds of millions of dollars' worth of needed humanitarian research and has led to important research breakthroughs on issues such as childhood brain cancer. It supports studies on Ebola, tuberculosis, and the Zika virus. World Community Grid is free. It provides massive supercomputing power via millions of connected devices. It created a meaningful social media network, intellectual capital, and a platform for building skills. Perhaps most important, it was developed at a time when governmental support for basic health care research was in decline and threatened with further reductions.

IBM's Corporate Service Corps—often referred to as the private-sector version of the Peace Corps—was launched in 2008. It has sent over one thousand teams of the company's best and most talented staff on monthlong assignments to 37 countries in Africa, Latin America, the Middle East, and Asia. One team created a plan to reduce mother-to-child AIDS transmission. Another created an integrated food bank network. And yet another instituted a detailed management system for a free health care program for poor women and children in Nigeria. None could have been achieved by the staff at NGOs or government programs working alone. It realized a triple benefit: creating a more skilled workforce, reducing attrition rates, and developing intellectual capital. It built skills in cultural adaptability. Most important, it provided over $100 million in benefits across the 37 countries at a time when government funding for international development was reduced.

Perhaps most significantly, in 2010 IBM began an effort to breathe new life into education reform by addressing the growing skills crisis. The education reform movement had become fractured, with forces on the political left and right in deep disagreement over funding, choice, charters, standards, teacher evaluation, and labor issues. Anger from all sides had already derailed implementation of Common Core academic standards. And companies interested in school reform could point to few scalable and sustainable reforms that had been inspired by their actions. Thus the creation of P-TECH, a reform of high school by combining high school and college as a path to twenty-first-century careers.

And finally, the role of artificial intelligence and big data in altering the social safety net and education is particularly intriguing and forward-looking. IBM's best researchers, working in collaboration with some of the nation's most gifted educators, created a game-changing use of technology called teacher advisory with Watson, a personalized coach assisting U.S. teachers in the teaching of math. This free resource offers teachers the ability to improve teaching practice and ultimately student achievement. This pathbreaking initiative also comes at a time when government support for education reform and change has been taxed. Support for sorely needed teacher professional development has been cut, and ways to reform career and technical education through significant and important action are not being addressed at either the federal or state level.

The most effective approaches to responsible corporate behavior must connect to business strategy and capability, but they must start with a set of core values. This is critically important to effective corporate responsibility. Those values must be embraced and understood at the CEO and senior executive level and transmitted down through management and employees. Things like a commitment to trust and personal responsibility, ethical behavior, and commitment to community are vital and are equally important to business success. And perhaps just as important, those values and the behavior that follows must be understood and practiced in a way that reflects the ability to collaborate and partner with government and civil society, melding corporate investments with those in the public and not-for-profit sectors working on the front lines. To do more than "give back" and achieve success it is important to understand that no company can achieve significant gains operating alone. The same is true of every sector of society. Education is but one example. All private contributions to education combined add up to no more than 1 percent of total spending. This drives home the point that real achievement is directly connected to effective engagement, which is connected to business success. Many of the examples cited in this book will connect directly to core values, and all that are successful will demonstrate the ability to engage closely and over time with partners, across all sectors of the economy, producing significant value and leading to sustainable and scalable results.

The message is clear: As governmental policy and pressures make it difficult to address challenges involving health or environmental research, international development, education reform, or support for cities, the private sector must step up and play a significant role not only in attempting to address gaps but also doing so in an innovative and effective fashion. But leadership by some does not and has not eliminated the bad business practices of others. An increasing number of companies are committed to operating in positive ways, but just as many do the opposite. Can we reconcile this type of good and bad behavior with the tone of the 2016 presidential campaign rhetoric that implies that all business activity is divorced from community needs and motivated solely by greed, and is focused on spreading income inequality more broadly? Is there a chance to break the cycle of some doing well while others do not?

Is it possible to diminish or eliminate some of the negative practices engaged in by so many? The actions of Enron, which participated in massive financial fraud, WorldCom, which defrauded its investors, Countrywide, whose lending practices contributed to the recession of the early part of this century, and of course the enormous fraud perpetrated by Bernie Madoff are examples demonstrating just the reverse of corporate responsibility. What these companies did is well known; it mirrored the actions of others in years past. Why they did it can be understood in one word: greed. How to prevent it is less well known. Companies behaving in this way created massive economic hardship as people lost life savings and gainful employment. There were some effective legal remedies and government prosecution, but the most effective way forward is prevention, not remediation. And this can only be done if we value ethics.

When we get past the numbers, these historical benchmarks reveal personal stories of leadership along with corruption. In this book we will attempt to outline both the positive and negative examples to learn from them. Of course, what they also demonstrate is that those behaviors could continue regardless of legislative or regulatory actions. Bad behavior spans decades and results from of a lack of ethics, lack of values, and a misunderstanding of sound business practices. These actions were motivated by greed, just as the positive actions were motivated by principles and strong values.

What can we learn from positive and negative behavior to root out the negatives and to advance, scale, and sustain the positives? Can we embed positive behavior messages and lessons in not just business schools, but all schools? Does ethics have a place in education, at all levels? Can we embrace real change? To proceed we need to start with the facts and a deep understanding of policy and each sector's role. But then we need to translate such an understanding of where we are today to where we can be in the future.

We often think of actions in the public sector as being separate from actions in the private sector. The same is true of civil society. Actually, a review of history demonstrates that the reverse is true. Government and business along with civil society have often been close partners in developing programs, strategies, and policies and then executing them. Business leaders have often helped launch not-for-profit entities, served on not-for-profit boards, and collaborated with business and government in a host of ways. When the sectors work together effectively, they are able to see greater success.

The Future Is in Our Hands—Don't Blow It

But the real reason for us to talk about past practices, good and bad, or current practices, negative or positive, is to learn as much as we can about why and how institutions behaved, both good and bad. But next is whether we can really afford a future that looks like our past. Or is there a way to completely alter the nature of corporate behavior? What do we know about the role of business and society going forward? What can we expect, or, better still, what can we do to chart a way forward that will discard the shackles of the past and give us the returns from business that will lead to economic success and societal improvements?

How can business address the global climate challenges or the growth in income inequality? Can business play a consistently positive role in addressing the skills crisis, the lack of high-performing schools, the need for an effective and more economical social safety net, and a broader understanding across culture and across geographies? Can this be done while business manages itself effectively and meets its business goals? Can business resources, political leadership, and the time and talent of their employees effectively address these issues? Can business work effectively with governments at the local, state, and national levels? Can civil society be more than just a place to donate excess cash? Can businesses' core values carry them through periods of change and technological disruptions? What role can business play in engaging civil society, and what change can we expect going forward? Can we craft solutions that are systemic, scalable, and sustainable, charting a path to the future that will demonstrate the effectiveness of corporate responsibility? Can we end finger pointing and promote collaboration?

A path forward ought to focus less on process and more on outcomes, with incentives and disincentives for performance. If we expect corporations to engage in more progressive labor practices, investing more in their employees and their communities, let's outline the outcomes we expect and assess and evaluate them against results, offering as much flexibility as possible in implementation. If we want to rein in corporate misbehavior, let's design the most effective ways to do so and put muscle behind it.

Do we have goals that can be quantified, do we have metrics that we can assess? If we expect more cross-sector engagement, and more effective mobilization of resources, let's think seriously about how this can result as well. Do we have the structures in place to encourage and assist in such engagement or do we need to operate differently? Do we need to examine governance structures, in government or the private sector, that might inhibit such engagement? We have always focused a good deal of attention on penalties for bad behavior, and rightly so, but have we really thought through and encouraged an intelligent reward system that would be needed to encourage good behavior and focus it on critical areas of need?

My cross-sector experience, beginning when I worked for a mayor, advised a governor, led a major nonprofit, managed the largest school system in the United States, and reshaped and sustained corporate responsibility at an iconic global business, has afforded me a unique opportunity and a unique experience to share a clear set of objectives and a road map to high-end performance.

Our future could be dim or bright, but only if we learn from the past, learn from the present, determine what works and what does not, and figure out what we can do to convert shared value into real value.

In the last part of this book we will chart a path for the future and the things that can be put into place that will make our future a bright one. We can go from risk to reward.

Chapter 1

The Good, Bad, and Ugly: A History of Corporate Behavior

In the late nineteenth century, Carnegie Steel was one of the world's most well-heeled and effective businesses, expanding its workforce in large numbers and growing rapidly across the United States. It came close to being a monopoly, and its success enriched its founder, Andrew Carnegie, who first gained prominence in the railroad industry. With the financial support of J. P. Morgan, Carnegie leveraged his knowledge and experience to build a massive business in steel, to the point where by 1885 he was producing most of the steel that built America's tools, factories, tall buildings, ships, streetcars, and machines. He was an iconic American business leader. Carnegie's personal wealth approached that of John D. Rockefeller, reaching far beyond any nineteenth-century standard of wealth. In today's world, Carnegie would be more than just a billionaire; his wealth would be at the Bill Gates or Warren Buffett level. To put the success of Carnegie's business into context, when he sold Carnegie Steel in 1901, it netted him nearly $500 million, which today would equate to more than $15 billion. And this was not value that would accrue to shareholders, investors, and executives; it represented Carnegie's personal enrichment, building on his already extensive wealth. And Carnegie's personal wealth grew subsequent to the sale, allowing him eventually to become one of the world's most generous philanthropists, on a scale equal to that of Rockefeller.

Carnegie didn't just give out money via his philanthropy. He had a vision of what he wanted and executed it effectively, pioneering America's public library system, which contributed to the nation's literacy and its transition from agriculture to a manufacturing-based economy. Carnegie's transformative private foundation survives to this day and plays a vital role in the support of public education and civil society. Its impact has truly been significant. Carnegie is a brand with strong positive impact. And yet the success of his company depended not a scintilla on philanthropy, sound business ethics, solid labor practices, or the support of community. Quite the contrary. Carnegie and the company he founded focused with laserlike attention on the economics of building and sustaining the business, which he did at any cost.

The company did provide benefits to the American economy. It pioneered steel production at massive levels, effectively competed with international geographies, and enriched a range of companies, including the railroads that it did business with. Most important, it created a large number jobs for Americans at a time when industrialization was on the rise. But in that period of industrialization, economic success depended heavily on the productivity of, and the company's relationship with its core asset, its workforce. Carnegie and the tight group of executives he had chosen to manage and lead the company in the late 1880s became increasingly worried and concerned about the influence of its fledgling labor union, the Amalgamated Steel Workers. The union representing these skilled workers saw the increasing size and scope of the company, and its astounding financial success, and saw an opportunity to increase wages, limit the workweek, and improve working conditions.

Work conditions at Carnegie's company were certainly not unique: it had a six-day and in some cases seven-day workweek, twelve- to fourteen-hour or longer workdays, unsafe working conditions, low wages, incidences of child labor, and offered no vacation days or overtime pay. This Industrial Revolution was a time of increased focus on working conditions and worker pay across American industries and around the world. This was intensified by an economic slump in the early 1890s that was part of a range of global economic trends largely beginning in Europe. Carnegie and his company chairman, Henry Clay Frick, who was in charge of the company's Homestead plant in Pennsylvania, felt the need to act and act promptly to reduce and not increase their labor costs. (Incidentally, Frick also donated his personal wealth at the end of his work life, in his case to create the Frick Museum on Fifth Avenue in Manhattan, which survives to this day.)

Carnegie and Frick and their tight circle of very well-compensated managers and investors were convinced that increased labor costs and any labor demands to improve working conditions and employee benefits would damage the fiscal future of the company and cut into the financial well-being of Carnegie Steel. This was top of mind to Carnegie because steel markets were in a brief decline. The consequences of their actions on the workforce were more than secondary, they were profound. As a result, in 1892 discussions with the union, Carnegie and Frick proposed not only to turn a deaf ear to any and all demands by the union, but to go one step further and reduce the minimum wage in the new contract. And beyond that, they aimed to abolish the bargaining power of the union entirely.

When the negotiations faltered, Carnegie and Frick ceased their negotiations with the Amalgamated Steel Workers and instead aimed to beat the union, or more explicitly, to break it. Their plan had nothing whatever to do with effective negotiation tactics, fairness, or even long-term success. They conceived and executed a strategy that began with employing hundreds of strikebreakers to replace the company's striking workforce; in record time, they built a ten-foot fence around the workplace to prevent interruption of work. But perhaps most important, they hired the Pinkerton Detective Agency to engage in swift, armed conflict with the strikers. The Carnegie and Frick strategy resulted in the deaths of dozens of workers, with over a hundred more injured, and effectively ended the worker strike and opposition to the company's labor practices.

They developed and executed their strategy swiftly and without remorse. The action effectively accomplished their goal—it broke the union. While Frick never regretted the action, Carnegie did. He later wrote, "No pangs remain of any wound received in my business career save that of Homestead." Perhaps some of his commitment to philanthropy served as a reaction to those events. However, in response to Carnegie's personal philanthropy in the creation of libraries, the president of Dartmouth College at the time, William Jewett Tucker, referring to Carnegie's efforts, opined that it was a "belated gospel . . . and too late for a social remedy," and one of Carnegie's steelworkers at the Homestead plant said, "What good are libraries to me, working practically 18 hours a day?"

Carnegie and Frick's reaction to their workers organizing to improve labor practices was not unique. The Pullman Strike in 1894, the 1902 anthracite strike, the 1913 Paterson silk strike, and the 1914 Colorado coal strike grew out of similar circumstances. Workers organized to improve working conditions and compensation, and in swift reaction employers beat back their demands with planned and calculated violence.

The actions that led to the Colorado strike and what happened afterward, known as the Ludlow Massacre, are particularly illustrative. Brooklyn-born John C. Osgood established a very successful mining company in Colorado called Colorado Fuel and Iron. Osgood has been characterized as one of a generation of business leaders known as the "robber barons." Though CF&I was actually owned in the main by John D. Rockefeller, Osgood played a major role in the company and had broad influence over the entire mining industry. Initially he seemed to be a progressive business figure, establishing the town of Redstone, Colorado, as a "company town" and investing in housing for its employees and even building a school for Redstone children and their parents. But after a strike by the workers, similar to what led to Carnegie and Frick's brutality, Osgood embarked on a publicity campaign to discredit the workers. He engineered actions by the National Guard to break the strike and break the union through violence. Two dozen people were killed in Redstone, leading to further violence. While the union was broken and these industrialists prevailed in the short run, a growing negative reaction by American citizens began to develop, leading to organizing and political advocacy at the state and national levels that ultimately brought about passage of child labor laws and the eight-hour workday.

Carnegie and Frick as well as Osgood and Rockefeller and many others were successful, at least in the short term. In the case of Carnegie and Frick, they and the company created some economic benefit, to be sure, but they enriched themselves greatly and cared little about the consequences. Carnegie's business grew rapidly through the end of the nineteenth century into the beginning of the twentieth. The business practices he followed with respect to his workforce were reprehensible. And, sadly, they had their influence on the practices of many other businesses. Jay Gould, a man of outsized wealth, legendary for his greed and lack of ethics, and importantly an investor in CF&I, summed up his views regarding labor practices as follows: "I can hire one half of the working class to kill the other half." Gould's actions went far beyond breaking unions. He engaged in stock fraud, manipulated the gold market, and rightly earned his membership in the club of robber barons.

These actions had an impact not only on business behavior but also on Americans' view of large companies and their business practices overall. America at that juncture was hardly pro-labor and certainly not pro-union, but the actions of Carnegie and Frick in their Pennsylvania steel plant and beyond were viewed negatively by most Americans and reinforced a view that wealthy business owners were singularly focused on greed and profit, regardless of the cost. Instead, those actions further spurred labor organizing efforts. Ultimately, they led to changes in government at both the state and federal levels to reverse conditions that in retrospect are embarrassing to all Americans. Between 1880 and 1900, 35,000 workers died in factories and mines as a consequence of unsafe working conditions. In the same period, another 500,000 were injured. With respect to child labor the numbers are even more distressing. By 1900, 1.7 million children under the age of 16 worked in factories and fields. And roughly 20 percent of all boys and girls across America between the ages of 10 and 15 worked long days in poorly compensated salaried jobs.

So clearly the actions of Carnegie, Frick, Osgood, Gould, and others were not unique, and they were not confined just to labor practices either.

Decades earlier, John Jacob Astor created the American Fur Company, which used intimidation and monopolistic practices to put his competitors out of business, cheated Native Americans, and thus grew his business and his personal fortune. His workers were paid and treated very poorly, and communities and competitors suffered greatly as a result. James Fisk, the founder of Fisk and Belden, controlled the Erie Railroad. By fraudulently inflating the price of gold, which led directly to the stock panic of 1869, and engaging in blatant stock fraud, Fisk increased his wealth and the wealth of his company, again at the expense of workers, communities, and investors. He actually swindled his investors and created and sold fraudulent stocks. At the same time on the West Coast, Leland Stanford, whose name is emblazoned on Stanford University and whose business school pioneered the teaching of both business ethics and corporate responsibility, served as the chairman of the Central Pacific Railroad. While today this would be inconceivable, at that time he led his company concurrent with his service as California's governor. In his capacity as governor, Stanford enriched his company and himself by combining state funding and state resources in service to the company. The growth of the railroad was achieved by seizing property via eminent domain claims, and by routinely making outsized cash donations to government officials to obtain ownership of property. He was able as a consequence to see his and his company's influence grow. The benefits to Stanford's company came at the expense of the public coffers and the communities he was elected to serve.

Such corporate practices not only negatively affected the employees of a single company, they had a broader negative effect on society. They hurt investors, defrauded the competition, and emptied governmental coffers. While there were clearly some immediate and short-term economic benefits to the companies, the practices wound up in the main costing jobs, and as a consequence had a negative overall societal effect. The labor practices of these companies were simply not sustainable. When these company practices became known, via news coverage by reporters who became known as "muckrakers," they affected the public's views about those individuals, their companies, and ultimately the private sector overall. The resulting negative consequences far outweighed the short-term benefits.

This group of late-nineteenth-century business leaders engaged in the antithesis of ethical business practices. As a direct response to such negative behavior, federal and state legislative action was initiated, with broad and growing public support, to curtail unethical business practices.

It began at the federal level, in the administration of President Theodore Roosevelt, who opined, "I believe in corporations. They are indispensable institutions ... but I believe they should be supervised and regulated, that they should act in the interest of the country as a whole."

Another Way of Proceeding

Teddy Roosevelt's attitude and the federal legislation he championed that followed have been extensively written about. The legislation was designed to rein in those corporations in particular and more broadly the private sector overall, altering corporate behavior over the long term. In the early years of Roosevelt's administration, the Department of Commerce and Labor was created (years later it was split into two cabinet-level agencies), and one of its key units was the Bureau of Corporations, which Roosevelt believed could monitor unethical and greedy business behavior and, by its very existence, avert it. Roosevelt continually used his presidential bully pulpit to decry unethical business practice and rein it in through legislation and regulation. His successor, President William Howard Taft, who had a far more pro-business attitude, also called for a focus on "fair dealing" on the part of business. Early on in his presidency, Taft even went so far as to encourage companies to offer paid vacations.

Regulations instituted by Roosevelt helped, without a doubt, and the focus on fair dealing and ethical practice made total sense, but neither actually solved the problem, and scandals and unethical practices persisted in the early decades of the twentieth century. However, what resulted from those scandals was a growing anger on the part of the public toward business leadership, or the lack of it, and it had its effect on governmental policies. And while Roosevelt and others hoped that their actions would significantly change corporate behavior over the long term, and unquestionably they were effective to some extent, at least in the short term they did not eliminate poor corporate behavior entirely, nor did they eliminate the need for further actions by government. In a speech before the U.S. Chamber of Commerce, which was founded in 1912 to give business a voice in governmental action, then secretary of commerce and future Republican president Herbert Hoover, who was also generally thought of as a strongly pro-business conservative, in a speech to corporate leaders said that "business must end its wrongs or law will."

Various forces, spurred on by advocacy efforts, progressive politicians, and labor organizers, attempted to turn their disfavor into legislation and regulations as a means of ending such bad practices. Muckraking investigative journalists were particularly effective in highlighting bad ethics and close-to-criminal behavior, stimulating such action. And it was not only investigative journalists who got into the mix profiling bad business behavior. Novels by well-respected writers like Upton Sinclair had an equally important impact. Sinclair's 1906 novel *The Jungle* outlined the horrendously unsafe and unsanitary conditions in the Chicago stockyards, and arguably led to the passage of the Pure Food and Drug Act. Ida Tarbell, the leading female journalist of the era, published a devastating set of pieces on John D. Rockefeller's Standard Oil Company, detailing a clear record of bribery, corporate espionage, and industrial deceit. While Tarbell's writing led to local and federal prosecutions of Standard Oil, and arguably led Rockefeller to pursue personal philanthropy to address the damage to his reputation and that of his company, his company's financial success continued and its unethical and decidedly antilabor practices went unchanged for years.

The Progressive movement was successful in electing to political office a range of important reformers, a clear reaction to bad business behavior. However, while such efforts were sorely needed and somewhat successful, they did not end or even diminish bad ethical practices or bad business behavior. In a relatively short period after the Progressive Era of the first years of the twentieth century, pro-business activities resurged in America in the 1920s, ushering in the Great Depression, which in turn demonstrated how much still needed to be done. The reaction and result to the Depression in the 1930s was President Franklin D. Roosevelt's New Deal. While it again led to a host of actions aimed at ending bad business practices, largely via legislation and regulation, it too did not end such behavior.

I could go on and on detailing the negative actions of business in virtually every decade of America's history, but it would be a mistake to paint every business leader and segment of the private sector with the same brush. The facts, the data, and a review of history, demonstrate just the opposite. Clearly the negative behavior of some business leaders, perpetuated by greed and a lack of ethics and responsibility, was not the direction followed by all. A review of history demonstrates how far from the truth such a statement would be.

Consider instead George Cadbury and his brother. In the late nineteenth century they built a successful candy company in England. It was a success, but by no means as successful as the efforts of Carnegie and Rockefeller in the United States, or even some of the best-known large-scale businesses in England. Yet by the 1880s, Cadbury grew substantially to nearly three thousand employees with multiple millions of dollars in revenue. The Cadbury brothers gained significant personal wealth, but as George Cadbury built his business, he also engaged in what would be described in today's terminology as innovative corporate social responsibility.

Cadbury understood that the success of his company depended largely on the productivity of his workers. To enhance their productivity, unlike the strategies employed by Carnegie, he created workers' councils for both his male and female employees, offering them a seat at the table with his managers to work with him and the company to develop sound and effective labor practices. It may sound simple, but he believed in listening to those in his employ. The outcome of those worker councils included both improved wages and improved employee benefits. With those improvements, Cadbury believed that worker productivity would increase, and without question it did as the company continued to grow and prosper.

Cadbury also helped develop a range of other progressive policies. To further address the financial needs of those in his employ, he helped to create affordable housing for his workers and engaged in what today would be called environmentally sound business practices as well. He received no governmental support for any of these activities, and none were mandated or required by government. But by providing his employees with affordable housing, safe working conditions, and a seat at the table in determining business practices, he believed that not only employee productivity would be enhanced but also community stability. The company definitely saw the benefits in its bottom line.

Cadbury, while a genuine leader and pathbreaker, was not alone. There was similar leadership in the United States. In 1875, the American Express Company established the nation's very first private pension plan for its employees. With the exception of veterans of the Revolutionary and Civil War, no pension plans existed for American workers, certainly not in government, and not in private business either. American Express pioneered this practice, offering employees with 20 years of service roughly 50 percent of their salaries in retirement at age 60. They did so as an employee benefit to improve worker productivity and raise the company's brand value with prospective employees. There was a cap on total benefits, but it was very forward-thinking and led to similar action by other companies in the later part of the nineteenth century.

Following the leadership of American Express, in the half century before the creation of Social Security, more than 420 American companies, including AT&T and GE, without being required to do so by a governmental entity, established and paid for their own private pension plans with no costs passed on to their employees. The Baltimore & Ohio Railroad, a competitor of American Express (which in those days was a railroad), provided 35 percent of salary for employees who retired at age 65 with 20 years of work history with the company. While B&O's plan was not as generous at the American Express pension plan, it was still at that juncture unusual. Perhaps this why American Express is still in business while B&O is not. Obviously in that era when life expectancy was roughly age 60 or 62, offering pension benefits to retirees was not overly costly to an employer. In fact, American Express's lifetime cap of $500 on its pension payout was thought of as generous, and it was a unique benefit that set the company apart. Clearly it had a cost, and that cost came out of company profits, but it was neither a legislated nor regulated policy, and it predated the creation of any public-sector pension benefit at the city, state, and federal levels by over half a century.

Eastman Kodak was another company that took great pride in its corporate practices and leadership. Founded in 1892, in the early years of the twentieth century it was growing its business and its reputation as a leader in both innovation in business practices and corporate citizenship. In 1919, the company's founder, George Eastman, gave a third of his holdings of company stock, at the time worth $10 million, to his employees. Shortly thereafter, Eastman made a gift of $10 million to the Massachusetts Institute of Technology (MIT), which he had not attended, and several years later established and paid for free dental clinics for children in Rochester, New York, funded through his own largess.

In today's dollars these contributions would be massive demonstrations of a company's commitment to its employees, to educational growth, and to communities.

Eastman himself, and then Kodak throughout the 1940s, '50s, '60s, and '70s, had exemplary labor practices, including a commitment to lifetime employment for his company's employees and strong and consistent support for the communities where it operated. It continued the tradition of a variety of exemplary corporate citizenship practices, especially in the Rochester community. An article in the *New York Times* in 2017 contrasted Kodak's labor and business practices and benefits to those of Apple. While Kodak may have experienced business challenges at the beginning of the twenty-first century, a review of company practices demonstrates that through the duration of its success and innovation as a company, its responsible business practices over many decades enhanced its business success.

Progressive actions were not restricted to manufacturers or industrialists. Health benefits, pioneered by labor unions like the Granite Cutters' National Union, which set up such benefits in the United States for its members in 1877, and spreading decades later to the members of the International Ladies' Garment Workers' Union, began to be embraced by certain private-sector pioneers as well. Some railroads hired physicians to provide free health services to their employees for work-related injuries, long before health care was widely provided by companies or by the government. And though some criticized the quality of such care due to the skills of those hired by the companies, it was still an innovative practice and unusual by virtue of the fact that it was provided at all. Macy's in the 1870s also pioneered activities in the health arena by providing health care to its employees. And International Harvester provided not only a sickness plan for its full-time employees dating to 1908 but also death benefits and disability benefits. There are ample examples of companies establishing a range of services in "company towns." George Pullman, for example, invested over $8 million and established a company town outside Chicago that offered its employees community facilities, recreational facilities, and company-supported housing. He was widely praised for such actions, but when the economic downturn happened in 1893, he cut wages while leaving the cost of rent in company-owned housing constant, and much of the positive attention he had received turned negative.

In 1914, Thomas Watson Sr., the chief executive officer of what became IBM, hired the company's first disabled worker. Two years later he established the company's Employee Education Department, followed by its Open Door Policy, which allowed any employee access to corporate leadership to challenge any company policy whatsoever, including its labor practices. In the 1930s, IBM instituted paid life insurance policies for its employees who had worked for the company for a year's time, along with survivor benefits for employee families and training programs for all its workers, including women and the disabled. And in 1953, more than a decade before passage of the Civil Rights Act, then CEO Thomas Watson Jr. issued a very specific equal opportunity policy letter outlining the company policy against any kind of racial discrimination in the workplace. Shortly thereafter Watson Jr. formally endorsed what he characterized as "wild ducks," those who were willing to challenge any and all company policies and procedures in innovative ways. While most of the work of these wild ducks was focused on commercial and business issues, there was ample attention paid to issues of corporate responsibility offering employees the ability to participate in, and in some cases actually shape, policy development in a range of areas affecting work life and the community.

Policies by IBM, Cadbury, American Express, and many others were not implemented out of anything other than a desire to build an effective and profitable company with loyal and productive employees in stable and effective communities. The companies' leadership showed a commitment to their employees. They also predated, and in many cases influenced, future governmental actions and societal changes because of the personal leadership of their corporate leaders. These companies, like Carnegie's and Rockefeller's in the nineteenth century, were successful, and in many cases very successful. But unlike the businesses of many of the robber barons, many of these businesses have sustained themselves and remain in place more than a century later. American Express has been in business for 150 years, and IBM and Cadbury for well over 100 years.

While they are certainly not perfect—and we could detail some of the practices that did not measure up to their own high standards of behavior—these companies were successful without incurring significant damage to the communities where they were established, quite the contrary. In fact, analysis and data reveal the extent to which these practices demonstrated success for both business and society. And while bad corporate behavior clearly led to reactive actions by government, history shows us that examples of good behavior, and specifically actions by a host of companies that predated governmental policy, law, or, regulation, in fact often led the government to model its policies and procedures after actions undertaken by those companies. And importantly, it caused government leaders and the public to view those companies positively, affecting their bottom line and creating positive views of the private sector overall. That positive view stimulated actions by government in those communities that encouraged and supported further business growth and stimulated government actions that benefited communities overall.

A case in point is the U.S. policy on overtime pay. In 1938, in response to the nearly decade-long Great Depression and based on pressure by organized labor and support by the progressives in federal, state, and local government, the Fair Labor Standards Act (FLSA) was enacted. The act formalized the 40-hour workweek and the concept of providing overtime pay at a higher rate for those who exceeded 40 hours. While some employers opposed the FLSA, believing it would cut into their profits, many others did not, largely because they had already embraced the 40-hour workweek along with overtime pay long before this law was enacted. IBM was one of those companies. In 1933, the company enacted a 40-hour workweek after considerable internal debate about instituting a number of practices designed to fulfill the goals of its leadership to improve worker productivity and to attract and retain skilled workers.

In 1934, IBM disbanded any factory work in which reimbursement was based on piecework, which was a very common practice in those days, putting in its place full-time employment and salaried status for its workers. In the case of overtime, the IBM employment policy provided one-and-a-half-time pay for any hour worked beyond the 40-hour workweek. And a few years later, in 1937, IBM instituted a policy of providing six paid vacation days on national holidays along with its previously provided one full week of paid vacation, thus granting roughly eleven vacation days to each employee. It also developed an education policy that provided the equivalent of company-created schools to expand worker skills and establish career ladders for its full-time workforce. IBM also reimbursed employees for continuing education. An examination of the IBM archives demonstrates that such policies implemented by the company, along with its health insurance program for all full-time employees, all predating any government legislation and regulations, were enacted because the company's management believed that such policies were part of a business strategy that would improve productivity and provide a competitive edge in both recruiting and retaining top talent. The results demonstrate that these decidedly progressive labor practices were very effective. And these actions, largely instituted in the 1930s, played a significant role in the economic growth of the company in the 1940s and throughout the second half of the twentieth century. There are many examples of other companies moving ahead of governmental action with regard to labor practices for their employees. In 1920, Chase Bank, which is now part of JPMorgan Chase, provided a group life insurance program for all of its employees, and included disability benefits. The bank followed roughly a dozen years later with a generous contributory pension plan, before Social Security was enacted.

Corporate actions and leadership to implement their own progressive labor practices were, as referenced earlier, designed and executed to produce long-term economic benefit for the companies. However, certain company actions, beyond labor practices, also influenced a broader set of societal actions and led to governmental changes. Driving this point home is the concept of public-private partnerships and cross-sector collaborations.

Some of these actions benefited both society and business. A classic example is the role that J. P. Morgan himself and key businesses played in resolving two massive economic declines in America. The first was in the 1890s when a decline in gold prices threatened serious economic distress, and then again in 1907. In both instances Morgan used his influence and the economic power of his business to preserve the economy and save jobs and resources. In the spring of 1907, starting in Europe, there was market turmoil as a result of a worldwide credit shortage. This all happened at a time when there was no U.S. Federal Reserve. Things were drifting in the wrong direction, and on August 10, 1907, the U.S. stock market crashed. The losses were estimated in the billions, which at that time represented a clear forecast of economic recession. While there were over 20,000 banks across the United States, there was no common reserve nor a coordinated financial management system.

By October 1907 the situation was significantly worse and required swift action. Morgan took the lead. He brought together at his home (what is now New York City's Morgan Library and Museum) the key players in the banking community to come up with a bailout strategy. By November 5 the crisis was averted and a solution was put in place involving shared risk and shared investment by America's business and banking community, with modest government assistance. While the Teddy Roosevelt administration was a partner, putting up $25 million, the amount of money and influence provided by the bankers was far greater. President Roosevelt, who in many other instances played a leadership role, was not the major player in this one. While he signed off on the deal, it was constructed by the private sector, which was also the largest financial participant. In the development of the deal, all parties deferred to J. P. Morgan. And it was not only the American budget crisis that Morgan helped resolve. He also provided credit via his company to help the City of New York avert bankruptcy by putting together a syndicate to buy over $30 million in city bonds. Morgan was a business executive with considerable business skills, an entrepreneur who had a significant hand in industries as diverse as banking, oil and gas, steel, and many others, and while his first priority was the success of his business and the growth and stability of the private sector overall, he also understood the importance of community stability and was a leader who played a significant role in preserving the U.S. economy through at least two extremely challenging economic crises.

This may be an early example of business leadership stepping in to resolve a budget problem in America's largest city, but it most certainly was not the last. When the city had a serious brush with bankruptcy in the 1970s and the federal government seemed to turn a deaf ear, leaders within the business community, working hand in glove with the leadership of the city's municipal labor unions, stepped in to help both the city and the state put together a bailout plan and execute it. This effort is credited to Felix Rohatyn of Lazard Freres, David Rockefeller, then at Chase, and others, along with labor leaders such as Victor Gotbaum and Al Shanker, and, of course, New York's governor, Hugh Carey. But they largely followed the example first set by J. P. Morgan of putting the city's future front and center and using their stature and skills to fashion a shared solution to a very serious problem. Rohatyn in particular continued his engagement with city policy and fiscal issues, and forged relationships not just with political leaders but with labor leaders too.

Public–Private Partnership Before the Phrase Was Coined

One classic example of public–private partnership that went beyond the impact on one company and affected society as a whole is revealed in the work done by IBM, in collaboration with the U.S. government, in the creation and implementation of Social Security in the mid-1930s. Frances Perkins, the U.S. secretary of labor and the first woman to serve in a president's cabinet, when she was interviewed by Franklin Roosevelt in his library on the second floor of the newly elected president's town house made it very clear that her acceptance of the cabinet position was contingent on Roosevelt's agreeing to implement what became known as Social Security. Her government experience in New York State, which had enacted progressive labor practices under Roosevelt's gubernatorial administration, laid the groundwork for what she hoped to do on a national level. Once elected, Roosevelt, with Perkins's help and that of many others, focused with laserlike attention on the political challenge and got the new law enacted. Suffice it to say there was significant opposition to this new government benefit, both by Republicans in Congress and some leaders in the business community. While some companies like American Express and IBM had their own pension plans, most did not. With a Social Security program, Roosevelt and Perkins, with the support of legislators and the general public, persevered and were ultimately successful in getting Social Security passed in 1935, ultimately with strong support in both the House and Senate.

In many ways, the passage of a law is the easy part of the process; it is the implementation that presents the true challenges, as has been proved with the Affordable Care Act, passed in 2010. It became very clear at the onset of Social Security that while the president had the political skill to pass the law, the U.S. government did not possess the technical or managerial expertise to bring this innovative and groundbreaking program to fruition. Clearly it was much more than an operational challenge. It required technical innovation as well. Perkins sat with her principal deputy, Arthur Altmeyer, and they wondered how they could possibly bring this dream of hers and the president's into being and do it quickly. A French expert who was among a range of consultants they approached was brought to Washington to advise them. Upon analyzing the problem and the law, he gave them his best advice. He said it in one simple phrase, delivered directly to the secretary—"It can't be done"—and he strongly advised them not to go forward and thus avert disaster. Having gotten this advice from many, Perkins would simply not take no for an answer. Social Security was her passion, and most certainly President Roosevelt would not back down either. Her next overture was to begin discussions with Tom Watson, the IBM CEO. Watson was someone she knew well from her tenure in New York State government.

Watson's advice was different from that of the French consultant. He acknowledged that it would be incredibly difficult to implement, but he felt that it was not impossible. He arrived at this conclusion after discussions with his research and engineering staff. Like the consultants brought in by Secretary Perkins, they too realized that implementing Social Security would require a level of innovation that did not exist at that time. The challenge was daunting: it required issuing social security numbers to 26 million American workers, employed by over 3.5 million employers. This would be a massive challenge. The management system would require 24,000 square feet of space, and not just any space. No currently constructed flooring could hold the quantity or the nature of technology that would be required. And it all needed to be invented and implemented in months, not years. Any delay would threaten the program's very existence.

Watson and his team believed that IBM could actually invent and produce a new, never-before-implemented piece of technology, which became known as the IBM 077 collator. Along with trained staff they could manage the implementation. But the development of such a device would be costly. While he had no contract nor funding agreement with the federal government, since IBM, like any other company, would have to respond to a competitive request for proposal with no assurance that IBM would win the contract to do the work, Watson decided to take a chance. It was a big chance. In today's parlance it would be called a "big bet" or a "moon shot." Watson conferred with his team and made the decision to invest company resources in the creation of the

077 collator machine even before they received any assurance they would win the contract via competitive bid. They proceeded with the best skill and talent of IBM researchers and engineers to create the collator and then incorporate its deployment into their plan to bring Social Security from idea to reality.

IBM delivered first the plan and then the product in response to the competitive request for proposal. While there had been no assurance when they submitted the bid, ultimately they won the contract to help the nation implement Social Security. The cost of the collator was not reimbursable under the contract. After the initial meeting between IBM and the Labor Department, Deputy Secretary Altmeyer stormed into Frances Perkins's office and exclaimed, "I think we found it!" Watson's risk and IBM's solution was implemented, and it worked. Because of IBM's innovation and investment, the solution for implementing Social Security was up and running within year one, realizing its promise. Americans' support for Social Security has survived over eight decades. At the act's twenty-fifth anniversary celebration, Secretary Perkins, in a video recorded to mark the occasion, opined, "There would not have been Social Security without IBM." The beneficiaries were the American public and the voters who continued to support Roosevelt and every other president who followed him and needed to commit to continuing Social Security.

IBM and Watson's leadership helped the government create a benefit that helped the United States through the Depression and helped U.S. workers through the twentieth century and beyond. But it had more than a societal benefit. It also created a new business opportunity for IBM that transformed and clearly benefited the company significantly, and not just in the short term. In fact, IBM's revenue increased by over 80 percent in the four-year period from 1935 to 1939, and in that same period the company's workforce grew from a little more than 6,000 employees to over 10,000 employees. The increase in revenue and the expansion of the IBM workforce directly connected to the 077 collator machine and IBM's expertise built through its partnership with the government had a significant economic impact. It required a skilled workforce and education systems; companies followed IBM's model with actions of their own. But IBM was the main private-sector beneficiary. It grew and expanded its entire supply chain, creating many more jobs and enhancing economic growth in a host of areas and in a multiple number of geographies. Watson's relationship with Roosevelt and Perkins was a close one and their public-private partnership hardly began and ended with Social Security.

Such partnerships were not just between the private sector and government. A decade later, in 1946, after a lunch between Tom Watson and academic leadership at Columbia University, which hosted IBM's first research laboratory on its campus in New York City, the company partnered with the university to create a new academic discipline, ultimately called computer science. The lunch, originally scheduled for an hour, lasted four hours. IBM was moving to embrace a new business model involving computer technology, and while there were academic disciplines connected to this work, whether engineering, physics, and the applied sciences, the idea of a new freestanding academic discipline focused on the science of computers did not exist. Investments by IBM, which included providing employees and executives to assist in developing and teaching courses, furnishing equipment and financial resources, and giving internships and faculty fellowships, were delivered in a coordinated fashion. IBM was joined by other companies as well, along with leadership in the higher education community, in a collaborative fashion to jointly develop an academic discipline connected to technology that fueled America's economic growth throughout the twentieth century and beyond. Computer science contributed markedly to those efforts. Today we see many states and localities putting their support behind computer science in K–12 schools.

At this time and since, companies have developed their own education and training programs, internal and external, along with tuition reimbursement policies for employees to enhance and build their skills at public and private colleges and universities. In the 2016 presidential campaign, candidate Bernie Sanders called for making college free. In two states, Tennessee and New York, their governors, Bill Haslam (Republican) and Andrew Cuomo (Democrat), respectively, instituted state programs and policies designed to make college free for some or all students. In Tennessee, Governor Haslam's program provides a free two-year college degree to all, and Governor Cuomo expanded the concept in his Excelsior Scholarship program providing not just free two-year degrees but also four-year degrees for college students based on income.

In its initial year, the New York State program is benefiting over 22,000 students. Other states, like Rhode Island, led by their governors, are considering similar actions. And yet more than 100 years ago it was companies, not states, that began developing their own tuition assistance and education programs, largely at company expense, and many also provided tuition assistance programs for both courses and full degrees that were directly connected to the employee's work responsibilities. As we will see in the next chapter on present exemplary practices, Starbucks has taken this effort to the next level. Companies also assisted education by in many cases shifting hiring requirements, first to require high school diplomas, and then by requiring college degrees for certain positions. Many companies still have policies to reimburse employees for tuition costs at 100 percent if the education program is tied to an employee's job and career.

Progressive policies in the area of labor practices, pensions, health insurance, vacations, and overtime, along with education and skills, don't even come close to telling the entire story of positive performance by business either. There are examples of companies that extended their practices at the nexus between corporate and community culture in social and civil actions. IBM provides another good example. In 1953, a dozen years before passage in the United States of the Civil Rights Act and before the Supreme Court ruled an end to "separate but equal" in the *Brown v. Board of Education* decision, CEO Thomas Watson Jr. released a letter to all employees stating the company's view on diversity and inclusion—that both were welcome. At roughly the same time, in the mid-1950s, Tom Watson Jr. was exploring the potential of locating manufacturing facilities in North Carolina and Kentucky. Both states at that time were segregated both in the workplace and in their education systems. Watson made it clear in correspondence and negotiations with the governors in both states that the decision regarding whether IBM would locate facilities in those states depended on the workplace being fully integrated.

After much negotiation and back-and-forth, including threats by Watson to locate in other states, IBM established a facility in what is now Research Triangle Park in Raleigh, North Carolina, and one in Lexington, Kentucky, which ultimately became the site where Lexmark computers were manufactured. All aspects of these IBM facilities were integrated. And so were the public schools in Lexington, in large measure due to the integration of IBMs workplace there. Watson's activities were not unique. There were others like IBM who had progressive policies regarding diversity and inclusion before federal or state legislative actions. However, others did just the opposite. U.S. Steel, for example, had a subsidiary in Birmingham, Alabama. In 1948, when a range of local organizations representing the needs and interests of the local African American community, which was suffering under the weight of discrimination and segregation, sought assistance from U.S. Steel, they received the following public response from the company: "Any effort by a private organization like US Steel to impose its views, its beliefs and its will upon the community would be repugnant to our practice and our constitutional concepts." Never mind that such policies were counter to the nation's beliefs.

Discrimination and Jobs Are the Same Issue

Americans who may have thought that racial relations were moving in the right direction were given a stark wake-up call with the violence in Charlottesville, Virginia, in August 2017 despite a range of positive inroads made in the previous decades. Many companies stepped forward to condemn the behavior of the white nationalists and bigots who demonstrated and engaged in violence in Charlottesville. Those that did not will be paying a price for their lack of leadership. However, leaders in the private sector stepping forward against racism and bigotry, while clearly not universal, is certainly not new.

While Tom Watson Jr. believed that integrating his workplaces made sense from a business standpoint, his leadership on race and ethnicity issues emanated from his own social and political views as well. In 1944, his father and IBM's then CEO became the first company and corporate leader to support the United Negro College Fund. In addition to his personal and corporate support for the civil rights organization the NAACP, he actively sought out support for the NAACP from other companies as well as IBM's clients, business partners, and others. And this was only the beginning. President John F. Kennedy and Watson's son and successor, Tom Watson Jr., had a strong personal relationship. Early in his presidency, Kennedy instituted what he called a Plan for

Progress, calling on all large companies to institute equal opportunity employment practices similar to IBM's. Pledges were made and signed by a range of companies, including IBM, and were countersigned by the vice president, first Lyndon Johnson and then Hubert Humphrey once he became vice president under President Johnson. Kennedy initially got pledges from 268 companies; from 1961 to 1963 a survey of about half of those firms who responded reported that full-time employment increased from close to 30,000 African American employees to nearly 43,000, an average increase of 13 percent over a two-year period. Watson was proud to report to the president that IBM had increased its number of African American IBMers by nearly 24 percent in the same period, and he went further, committing that the progress the company made would not only continue but increase.

However, while he did not communicate this to the president, Watson was far from satisfied with the company's progress. Each quarter his top-tier officials in personnel reported to him their progress in meeting goals under the Plan for Progress, and in each quarter, he responded by outlining his dissatisfaction with their progress, challenging them to do more and to do it quickly. For example, IBM in New York City created a work-study program for high school students, providing part-time jobs during the school year and full-time employment in the summer where students also did classroom work. Participants were paid competitive wages for both. In 1966, fifty students were in the program and nearly all were promised jobs at IBM.

Watson congratulated his team on their progress, but he was adamant and insisted that the program could expand and achieve much better results with more effort. When they reported they were doing orientation sessions at high schools in Manhattan to encourage students to participate, he instructed them to do such sessions at high schools in all five boroughs of the city, not just Manhattan. Initially they resisted, but then complied. Shortly thereafter they reported on success at Evander Childs High School in the Bronx and then other high schools as well. Watson was relentless in pushing his team. It was clear to everyone engaged that this was a top priority of the CEO of the company, and they worked hard to impress him. To be sure, he wanted to impress President Johnson, and to position the company as a leader with the administration, but he personally believed in the goal and was relentless in the pressure he put on his staff to deliver better results. While a review of IBM during this period demonstrates that top human resources officials were engaged, Watson's consistent personal leadership was key in elevating this issue and ultimately producing a higher level of results. Given how embarrassing the lack of performance in the area of diversity has been to Silicon Valley in the twenty-first century, the example of Watson's personal leadership a half century ago is instructive.

Watson Jr.'s relationship with President Kennedy and, after Kennedy's assassination, with his brother New York senator Robert F. Kennedy, led to IBM opening a manufacturing facility in the Bedford-Stuyvesant section of Brooklyn in the late 1960s. At that point Bedford-Stuyvesant was not the only depressed neighborhood in the city, but arguably it was the most economically depressed and crime rates were skyrocketing. Its African American population was larger and more economically depressed than any other predominantly African American community in the entire city. Within its first year of opening, IBM's Bedford-Stuyvesant plant had 300 employees and in two years' time had more than 400, with three-quarters of the managers at the plant being people of color. By 1979, eleven years after first opening, the rented facility at Gates and Nostrand Avenues could no longer accommodate the number of employees, and it was relocated to a 168,000-square-foot facility at Nostrand and DeKalb Avenues. At its peak, the plant provided nearly 40 percent of the power for all IBM facilities across the United States, with the largest percentage of product being shipped to IBM's Poughkeepsie plant roughly 90 minutes north of the city. In 1993, roughly 25 years after the initial plant opened, the IBM Bedford-Stuyvesant plant was transferred to a company led and managed by IBM employees. That company survives to this day, with offices in Brooklyn and New Jersey.

In retrospect, it is important to step back and take a comprehensive look at IBM's and Watson's actions with respect to employment and diversity. Perhaps it is wise to go back and examine the specific language contained in the 1953 directive that Watson sent to all IBM employees. He was very clear in that directive.

Under the American System, each of the citizens of this country has an equal right to live and work in America. It is the policy of this organization to hire people who have the personality, talent and background necessary to fill a given job, regardless of race, color or creed. If everyone in IBM who hires a new employee will observe this rule, the corporation will obtain the type of people it requires, and at the same time we will be affording an equal opportunity to all in accordance with American tradition.

In addition to IBM's actions on diversity internally beginning in 1953, Watson also pioneered external programs, including scholarship programs through the United Negro College Fund, and building and maintaining a nationwide network of job training programs in partnership with the Urban League, sustaining it over a quarter century. In the twenty-first century, IBM launched the P-TECH program across from Albany Houses in Brooklyn, which largely serves a student population of low-income African American youth (coincidentally within walking distance from that old IBM plant in Bedford-Stuyvesant). It provides employment and paid internships, mentors, and other services, fulfilling Watson's legacy. I'll discuss more about this groundbreaking initiative in the sections of this book about the present and the future.

But in the mid-twentieth century, Tom Watson Jr. worked closely with top figures in government in a range of other areas. IBM worked very closely with the Kennedy administration beginning in the early 1960s on the space program, and IBM's partnership with NASA in the race to put a man on the moon is a story in and of itself. A small glimpse of it was told in the 2016 film *Hidden Figures*, but the story goes well beyond what was revealed in the film. In addition to providing computers and consultants, IBM sent massive amounts of resources and engineering staff to NASA to partner with the government, much of it at the president's urging. In fact, President Kennedy was so close to Watson Jr. that he tried his best to get him to agree to be the Democratic candidate for governor of New York to run against then governor Nelson Rockefeller.

While the president was not successful in getting Watson to enter politics via the elected route, which may have been a very wise decision on Watson's part, his later decision with Robert Kennedy's urging to locate an IBM plant in Bedford-Stuyvesant had far more influence and over a longer period of time. And while Watson Jr. rejected Kennedy's plea to run for governor, he was later appointed U.S. ambassador to the Soviet Union by President Jimmy Carter in the late 1970s at a critical juncture in U.S. foreign relations, and his brother Arthur Watson, who headed

IBM's global operations, also accepted an ambassadorship. And clearly IBM was not the only company speaking out and demonstrating their position with respect to diversity and inclusion. In a survey conducted in 1973 by Eilbert and Parlet of literally hundreds of business leaders asking them to detail what they thought were the highest-priority issues with respect to corporate social responsibility, support for education was number three on the list, a focus on environmental practices was number two, and by the widest margin minority hiring was number one. In fact, 100 percent of respondents ranked it the top priority. Of course, identifying it as priority number one and addressing the gap in hiring based on race or gender is another story entirely, but the heightened interest and leadership demonstrated by some, along with political leadership, resulted in some changes in behavior.

Gender Equality

IBM's commitment to gender equality is also important to review in a historical context. It was in 1935 that IBM had its first class of women, both college and high school graduates, in its sales school in New York City, a rigorous two-month program. The initial class of 35 women joined 52 men, and later that year in an article in the *New York Sun*, with a headline saying that IBM was beginning a "pioneering program," Watson Sr. is quoted as saying that "men and women will do the same kind of work for equal pay. They will have the same treatment, same responsibility and the same opportunity for advancement." Of course, as with race, addressing the gender issues in the workplace would not and could not be addressed in one program or one announcement. By the 1960s, the percentage of women in the workforce lagged disturbingly behind, even though IBM did better than most large companies and was proud of the fact that 15 percent of its workforce were women. Decades later, Watson Jr. knew that much more needed to be done. In August 1970, thirty-five years after IBM's first sales school class of women, he sent a memo to all his managers with a clear message.

> This month marks the fiftieth anniversary of women's suffrage and yet securing equal rights for women is still a national social issue. Twenty five thousand IBMers are women and in the last five years

management positions for women at IBM has grown twice as fast as the company itself. However women are still disproportionately outnumbered in management and other key positions. Look at your own attitudes. You might have one of these notions . . . women lack ambition, women lack competitiveness, women fold under pressure, women are good at details but not bigger issues . . . any of these judgements can apply to any woman, or any man. They apply to all women as a group only in folklore. That folklore has no place in IBM. It undercuts our belief in the individual and our commitment to pay and promote on the basis of performance and merit.

As he did with the issue of racial diversity, Watson persisted in doggedly pushing his managers to execute his wishes and the company goals and in that same year appointed a corporate officer in charge of women's equal opportunity. And again, after memo after memo detailed progress, Watson consistently wrote back to his human resources executives demanding higher levels of performance. Of course, history shows that activities like this did not address the issue of gender equity completely. Far from it. In that same period the employment sections of newspapers across the United States advertised jobs for men and women separately. It was not uncommon for women to be let go when they became pregnant. The gender pay gap became a persistent American problem across sectors of the economy, and remains so today. However, as with the issue of race, early progress on gender equity came as a result of business leadership, and that leadership started at the top.

Environmental Leadership

Another important example of corporate responsibility can be found in the area of the environment and sustainability. The environmental movement began to take shape in the United States in the mid-twentieth century, with a good deal of advocacy and citizen activism taking place in the 1960s. This is not to say that there were not environmental activists and governmental and business leadership on these issues in prior decades; there most certainly were. The movement that created the national parks, protections for public spaces, and other environmental issues has its roots in the presidential leadership of Theodore Roosevelt. And yet it was in the 1960s and '70s that the most aggressive governmental embrace of environmentalism involving issues like clean air and water took place. Through Republican president Richard Nixon, urged on by Democrats in both the House and Senate, a cabinet-level agency, the Environmental Protection Agency (EPA), was created in 1970, and throughout the '70s federal laws and regulations were put in place to address the environmental risks of corporate practices in almost every industry. In 1972, there was the Federal Water Pollution Control Act, and in 1976, the U.S. Resource Conservation and Recovery Act, governing the disposal of solid and hazardous waste. It was followed in 1979 by federal action phasing out most uses of PCB, a harmful chemical compound used in electrical equipment, plastics, and various other industrial applications. Such legislation begat regulation and enforcement at local, state, and federal levels.

Many companies fought hard against these policies because they would be required to alter their manufacturing processes and procedures and reshape what they did and how they did it, thus incurring added expenses. Many companies that responded too slowly became targets of the EPA and wound up paying increasingly large penalties for their lack of action. Others invested heavily in legal actions challenging both laws and regulations, while still others spent heavily on lobbyists to influence policy and political campaigns at the federal, state, and local levels.

But others saw the changes as an opportunity to mitigate risk and obtain reward. In 1971, IBM issued its first corporate directive on solid waste disposal, followed one year later by company requirements for hazardous waste disposal. In 1973, it developed a global energy conservation program with specific metrics around environmental impact. Pro-environmental activity increased in the 1980s and '90s. In 1995, for example, IBM began to voluntarily report greenhouse gas emissions, setting very concrete and specific year-by-year goals for energy reduction along with emission reduction targets. The company prided itself on its environmental performance and was proud to report on its many awards, including a gold medal from the World Environmental Center in 1990, and became one of the first companies to participate in the EPA's voluntary toxic reduction program.

Certainly, IBM's environmental actions and performance were not perfect. In 1977, after groundwater contamination was discovered at one of IBM's manufacturing sites, the company began to aggressively monitor groundwater quality at all of its manufacturing and development locations worldwide. At places where solvents were discovered in the groundwater, IBM, like other companies with a history of manufacturing, determined to undertake aggressive remedial actions. Although the company cannot change or alter whatever might have led to such circumstances in prior decades, it did display a significant commitment to facing its remediation responsibilities fully in the following decades.

Johnson & Johnson is another company that was out front on environmental performance monitoring and reporting long before government requirements were in place. Johnson & Johnson began setting environmental goals as a company in 1990. Independent reviews have graded it along with European companies like Novartis and Novo Nordisk, and other U.S. companies such as Abbott, as significantly ahead of the curve with respect to their environmental performance and the quality of their reporting. Johnson & Johnson's founder, Robert Wood Johnson, took the lead in 1943, as Tom Watson did before him, in personally helping to craft the company values, which he characterized as the company "credo." It outlined its goals and responsibility to its employees, communities, and shareholders with a very simple narrative: "Put the people we serve first."

A classic example of environmental leadership was pioneered by another company, 3M. In 1975, 3M created Pollution Prevention Pays, challenging all of its employees across the globe to identify and then execute pathbreaking environmental projects endorsed and fully funded by the company. This effort has now been in place for over 40 years and demonstrates true environmental leadership. Literally thousands of projects were conceived by 3M employees, and then fully funded and implemented by 3M's gifted technical staff. While most of the projects affected 3M plants and facilities in the United States, it is now truly a global program that has saved the company well over a billion dollars, demonstrating the return on the company's investment. But more importantly it developed and reinforced environmental leadership at 3M and beyond through their innovation producing positive societal effects. In one project in Alabama, a 3M employee developed an effort to clean the cooling water at that plant and substantially scaled down the wastewater treatment facility. This saved the company nearly a million dollars and conserves water for the company and the larger community.

Often companies shift their understanding and response in their approach to environmental policy and practice based on various internal and external factors. Case in point is the experience of Dow Chemical. Founded in 1897 and headquartered in Midland, Michigan, Dow is a very successful company. It employs over 50,000 people, does business in 160 countries, and has a diverse set of businesses involving a range of what are characterized as "advanced materials," meaning involvement in energy, health, nutrition, agriculture, and transportation via a range of chemicals. During and after the Vietnam War, Dow was identified with two serious problems that threatened the company. One was its role in the creation of Agent Orange, the chemical compound dropped in Vietnam that devastated that country's environment and citizens. Closer to home was the dioxin controversy, which polluted the water near the company's Michigan headquarters.

Instead of hunkering down, fighting the charges, investing in lawyers, and deploying marketing and communications efforts in order to protect its brand, Dow determined to take another route. Dave Buzzelli, one of its executives and a Canadian, took a hard look at what had happened and reported to the company leadership that Dow suffered from a lack of trust. At that time, in order to get a better and more current view of the company facilities, the federal Environmental Protection Administration attempted to get access to the company via a "flyover" of the company facilities, which the company resisted. Buzzelli brought the decision to the highest level of the company and got it reversed. He believed that taking an adversarial stance on this issue would disadvantage the company in the long run. In 1990, he pulled together what became known as the Sustainability External Advisory Council, or SEAC. Dow determined to run each and every effort by SEAC, which was made up of environmental experts and advocates. With their help it developed 10-year goals to improve the company's environmental performance.

One thing the company was determined to take on was the issue of how it dealt with waste. It was that problem that wound up affecting water quality near Midland. Instead of dumping waste, Dow determined to incinerate it. And even though it was costly, that practice reduced significantly the waste that Dow needed to dispose of. The company brought members of SEAC to tour its incineration plant with great pride and were astounded when the response was not positive. SEAC encouraged the company not to incinerate waste, but to eliminate it. While this increased costs even more, the company embraced that recommendation and many others as well.

At the end of those 10 years the company could take pride in some startling achievements. They had more than 10,000 fewer leaks, reduced solid waste by over 1.6 billion pounds, reduced water use by 183 billion pounds, and saved 900 trillion BTUs (energy use). As a result, over 13,000 employees avoided injury. And it led to a next-phase 10-year plan, which has resulted in similar metrics and positive benefits for the company. It is a record that the company is rightly proud of, and yet what is perhaps most important is that the company saw its activities as essential in avoiding risk and increasing reward to the company. Dow learned a lot from what it did, and importantly how it did it. And in response, Dow management altered both the company's strategy and practice for executing against that strategy, engaging constituents in meaningful ways, and applying the same degree of innovation and attention to this issue as they did to their core business. Dow is not the only company to have embraced this approach, but its actions have been captured in a Harvard Business School case, so many future business leaders will learn the benefit of altering their practices and embracing environmental leadership.

Supply Chain Practices

In yet another example, decades ago many companies began to better monitor their supply chains, especially in the developing world, demanding that their contractors embrace environmental policies similar to the company's policies (as well as follow practices focused on better labor practices, especially child labor or labor policies based on sex or ethnicity). In 1972, IBM developed a supplier environmental evaluation program to determine suppliers' compliance with IBM's environmental guidelines. In 1991, it expanded the supplier evaluation program to include both recycling and disposal, an issue that had engendered a good deal of support from environmental advocates who focused on the computer industry. In the 1970s and 1980s, as companies began negotiating with suppliers around the world, they thought largely about the price and performance of a vendor providing goods and services, and most thought little about how products were made, how the vendor's employees were treated, or the overall policies and practices of the contractor.

Another company at the forefront of activities with its supply chain is the retailer Patagonia. As a matter of principle, it only purchases cotton from those who engage in organic farming policies and practices. It does this not because it was urged to do so, but because it felt doing so would increase the value of its brand, appeal to its customers, and ultimately is in its business interest to do so.

Things began to change in the late 1990s. As a consequence of global advocacy on the part of not-for-profit organizations and social responsibility advocates, focus was placed on the practices of a company's supply chain and not only its own practices. This led companies that had developed their own values and codes of conduct to make decisions to expect adherence to those principles by their contractors as well. These involved not only child labor practices but also working hours, wages and benefits, freedom of association, health and safety, environmental practices, ethical practices, and compliance with law and regulation. Step one was to get a company's suppliers to sign such a pledge. That was the easy part. The next step involved a way of effectively managing such a process, and by the early 2000s companies began performing independent audits on their supply chains and then working with suppliers who violated their pledge to either improve or lose their contract with the company. In 2004, IBM called together a range of companies in the information technology industry and initiated and led a joint industry group. The focus was on the development and implementation of a business model for supply chain practices that could be adopted industry-wide, including seeking broad support for the practice of independent third-party audits of company supply chain practices.

Independent audits are critically important. IBM, for example, supported audits in countries like China, India, Mexico, the Philippines, and Thailand, and also in Brazil, Hungary, Poland, and Romania. The results of the studies demonstrate their usefulness. In areas like ethical dealings, forced and child labor, and nondiscrimination, audits conducted over a 10-year period showed that contractors were between 90 and 100 percent compliant. However, in areas like wages and benefits, work hours, and health and safety, compliance rates were considerably lower, necessitating training and ultimately action against noncompliant suppliers, including barring them from continuing as suppliers. Clearly these positive examples of leadership affected business practices by others. However, we ought not think that it eliminated bad behavior. It did not. In the 1970s, the Ford Motor Company rushed its Pinto model onto the market to compete with Volkswagen's growing edge in the market, but the product was unsafe and ultimately caused Ford a great deal of economic pain. In the early 1990s, Sears pushed its auto mechanics with a goal of producing $147 worth of hourly benefits, which led to rampant overcharging of their customers. To this day, many companies have been held to account for negative practices by their contractors.

Lessons Learned and Strategies Used

What we can learn from a historical view of corporations and their role in society is this: there are examples of both good and bad business behavior, and they run across the totality of America's history. Some are about a single company engaging in bad behavior, like Carnegie Steel or Colorado Fuel and Iron in the nineteenth century, or recent twenty-first-century examples like WorldCom, Wells Fargo, Volkswagen, Enron, and Tyco. The result is anger in the public for the harm they cause, and often it leads to legislation or regulation designed to curtail such behavior. But there is always the other side of the coin where demonstrating good behavior, as exemplified by American Express, Cadbury, Dow Chemical, JP Morgan, Johnson & Johnson, 3M, IBM, and many others results in positive action and positive business results.

There are examples about an entire industry gone wrong, like the tobacco industry that asked Americans to discard all the research that demonstrated that smoking caused cancer and instead embrace tobacco and cigarettes, claiming they were manufactured with tobacco that was "toasted" and approved by doctors. This was a lie. After the recession of 2008, focus was turned on finance companies and hedge funds for fraud and insider trading, but criticism of Wall Street and financial firms goes back over a hundred years. Often the good and bad behavior can share the same year, the same decade, the same industry. What we can also learn is that America's views of business behavior wax and wane. There are periods where business can seemingly do as it pleases with little or no consequences, like in the 1880s. But these are followed shortly thereafter by far better business practices, such as the onset of the Progressive Era where robber barons and bad business practices were excoriated. Business largess in the 1920s resulted in the stock market crash of 1929 and the beginning of the Great Depression, and reactions to the stock market crash led to antibusiness attitudes and regulatory responses in the 1930s, during the period of the New Deal. America's business growth post–World War II into the 1950s led to pro-business governmental and societal attitudes. And the growth of business also produced higher tax rates to pay for investments in infrastructure, including America's highway system. In fact, in reaction to an economic slump at the end of the 1950s, a newly elected Democratic president, John F. Kennedy, in 1960 pushed through large-scale business tax cuts that successfully grew the economy. But this action, in addition to a range of other factors, also brought about the 1970s and a regulatory push in environmental standards, civil rights enforcement, and other areas. In the 1970s, we even had a Republican president, Richard Nixon, enact wage and price controls in the early part of the decade. In the 1980s during the Reagan presidency, for some Americans business could do no wrong. It was during that decade that a very popular television commercial publicized the slogan, "When EF Hutton talks, people listen." That pretty much sums up the attitudinal change toward business during the 1980s, though ironically EF Hutton shortly thereafter went out of business.

It is very clear from a fact-based review of history that the American view of business can shift and oftentimes concurrently runs both positively and negatively. How do we reconcile the good and the bad behavior? Can we expect that today's negative view of business, embodied in the phrase "income inequality," will simply run its course and in a decade or more will simply be reversed when it's clear that rhetoric alone does not result in behavioral change? The lesson of history tells us that this is likely to be the result. If the past is prologue to the future, then it is clear that if nothing changes, we can expect the past to repeat itself.

History tells us that the goal of responding to changes in America's views of business by attempting to alter business behavior through legislation and regulation has its strengths but also its weaknesses. Of course, this is true of any legislation or regulation, and it goes beyond efforts to change business behavior via legislation.

The stock market crash of 1929 influenced the next presidential election in 1932, bringing in Franklin Roosevelt and eventually the New Deal, but it also spawned a range of legislative and regulatory actions that attempted to control bad business behavior. It was such behavior in the decade preceding the crash that had led to the debacle. But the results hurt the vast majority of Americans, killing businesses and wiping out jobs. Between 1929 and 1932, there was a decline of about 80 percent in the value of stocks, and Americans' views of business, and Wall Street companies in particular, tanked. A host of high-profile cases of corruption followed, and in 1933 Congress, at the urging of the president, created both the Securities and Exchange Commission and the Federal Deposit Insurance Corporation, and in the same year passed the Securities Act, requiring that sales of securities be registered with the Federal Trade Commission. While it was fairly benign, a year later Congress passed the Securities Exchange Act, establishing the SEC and for the first time giving the government the power to regulate the stock exchange and prohibit manipulative trading. The Fair Labor Standards Act, which was enacted in 1938, was also effective in reining in bad business practices and went far beyond the issue of Wall Street and the stock market. American business unsuccessfully opposed most, if not all, of these actions, but ultimately learned to live with them, though it took the Second World War and the end of the Depression to reverse Americans' negative views of business and lead to the pro-business environment of the 1950s.

The more recent Foreign Corrupt Practices Act, enacted in 1977, addressed some of the most unethical business practices. This piece of legislation had a direct connection to actions that remind us of the worst kind of corporate behavior.

United Brands, whose predecessor company, the United Fruit Company, owned the Chiquita Banana brand, was led in the early 1970s by Eli Black, a former Lehman Brothers executive. Black orchestrated the merger that led to the creation of United Brands. In his letter to the company shareholders just three years later he boldly talked of the good morals of the company. An article in the *Boston Globe* stated that "it may well be the most socially conscious American company in the hemisphere." In this period many of the Central American countries where United Brands secured its fruit determined to create what emerged as the equivalent of a cartel to control their markets by raising tariffs on bananas specifically. This represented an economic challenge for United Brands. Their response turned out to be a huge mistake.

In a meeting that was ultimately chronicled in a government investigation, a United Brands executive had a meeting with the Honduran economics minister in 1974 in Miami, Florida. The executive representing Black and the company sought to find out what it would take to eliminate the tariffs. The minister was receptive and asked for a $5 million bribe to push repeal of the tariffs. Since the sum was so large, the executive needed to get the approval of his CEO. And with said approval, the company made the initial payment of $1.25 million through the company's European subsidiary and via a numbered account at Credit Suisse in Zurich, Switzerland, in order to avoid detection.

This overt act of bribery might never have come to public attention, but shortly thereafter Eli Black committed suicide by jumping out of the window of the company offices in what was then the Pan Am Building near New York's Grand Central Station. Black's suicide drew the attention of the U.S. attorney's office. But soon after the investigators began their work, the act of bribery surfaced. Ultimately the company, then led by investors who acquired the company after Black's suicide, settled the case in court, pleading guilty on six counts and paying a fine of $15,000. The U.S. Congress referenced the case of United Brands in 1978 when it passed the Foreign Corrupt Practices Act. Subsequent to the passage of the act, the illegal practices of a range of companies were prosecuted, leading to severe fines and penalties. Prosecutions peaked during the Obama administration. The actions of the Central American countries that raised their tariffs to pressure global companies were reminiscent of the actions of OPEC countries in their efforts to control the price of oil in the Middle East, but the response by Eli Black and his company, paying bribes, had its cost, and businesses, not just United Brands, suffered the consequences.

Most Americans believe that government is the primary regulator, and business its prime or principal target. Yet it is often government itself that is the entity regulated by other levels of government. Cities and counties are regulated by the state, and the state is regulated at the federal level. Some of those laws and regulations make sense, while perhaps others do not. And not-for-profit organizations that often contract with government to provide services are also controlled by law and regulation, some of them effective while some are not.

For example, the federal government tried to control job training activity conducted by local governments via legislation and regulation in the 1970s and '80s. In the midst of the 1970s recession and period of economic stress, a Job Training Partnership Act (JTPA) was passed, designed to disburse funding to states and localities for job training and placement services. But in an effort to ensure accountability for the allocated funds, job training agencies were to be judged by their effectiveness in providing services to those who actually got jobs. This meant that funding would depend on placement rates. If 70 percent of those receiving job training were placed in jobs, the program did well and continued to get funding. If only 40 or 50 percent of those receiving training found jobs, the program lost funding. Since the goal of job training is to get people jobs, this seemed to make sense. However, as it played out, it was deeply flawed. Since high placement rates protected funding and low placement rates did just the opposite, the act led to what is characterized as "creaming," meaning that services were only provided to those most likely to find work, and those who needed more education, training, or services to be connected to gainful employment, were driven out. This resulted in an underclass that desperately needed services in order to get employment not even being served. And while ostensibly the law resulted in higher placement rates, it failed to serve those most in need and created costs in many other ways

Another example involves the not-for-profit child welfare sector. Foster care agencies serve a population of young people who, through no fault of their own, have no reliable family, and those agencies operate facilities serving that population. The government, to ensure that reimbursement for services was appropriate, allowed agencies to receive additional funding based on the problem levels of the children and youth in their care. Agencies hired staff and directed them to document the children in their services as having significantly greater problems than they really had in order to receive higher reimbursement. The flaw was that case records, which followed each child throughout the system, led to children being inappropriately labeled, and it would end up being more of a problem than a solution, leading to lower not higher outcomes. In addition, while the write-ups of the children identified severe problems, many of them overstated, they did not correspond to the actual delivery of services designed to address the problems outlined. While providing services to children in foster care is critically important, this type of regulation defeated its purpose.

While these examples of the JTPA and foster care agencies don't have anything to do with business, they demonstrate that even what might appear to be a commonsense approach to either legislation or regulation in reaction to poor performance, the regulation or contractual requirements put in place might not accomplish the intended results and in some cases could exacerbate the problem and the cost of addressing the issue in both the short and long term.

Can We Intelligently Regulate Business?

Most of the examples of efforts to regulate business are issue-specific—environmental regulation, for example, as well as labor practices or diversity. One major act, in 1977, the Foreign Corrupt Practices Act, described above, made it illegal for companies to influence foreign officials with either payments in advance or rewards after the fact. This was instituted after evidence was collected demonstrating that over 400 U.S. businesses had made illegal payments totaling well over $250 billion to foreign governments. Lockheed was one public example, involved in a $12 million bribery scandal, and Chiquita was another. Since the Foreign Corrupt Practices Act was implemented, companies caught violating the law have seen penalties imposed, including prison sentences. Many companies have taken this law very seriously, instituting mandatory training programs for their employees and executives. During the Obama administration, there was heightened government enforcement of this act and an increase in penalties under the law. However, while it prevented and penalized inappropriate and illegal behavior to some extent, the act did not eliminate such actions altogether and likely never will.

One example of attempting to control business action via legislation occurred in South Africa. A law was passed mandating that companies awarded government contracts be owned by a percentage of black South Africans. The goal was economic growth and empowerment.

The result was that many companies created shell companies involving their own employees and obtained contracts and subcontracted with other companies. They got the government business but accomplished none of the desired goals. In the United States, this has been a way for some companies to game the system of preference for women- and minority-owned businesses.

The bottom line is that the legislator or regulator can only be effective if they can truly understand the entity they want to regulate, and the practice or behavior they need to alter. Otherwise, they run the risk that even the most reasonable goals will not be achieved and perhaps produce unintended negative consequences. Here again we have a lesson drawn from history. At a 1912 conference in Washington, D.C., at the Willard Hotel, President William Howard Taft spoke to a business audience, and as a result the U.S. Chamber of Commerce was created. His remarks could have been made in 2012. President Taft said:

> Even regulatory measures which have been adopted in the past may have suffered for lack of advice from those who should be best qualified by experience and training to give it . . . to that end you and the government must cooperate.

Legislation and regulation can only do so much. Instead, a study of business history allows us to focus on three other strategies designed to positively impact on the behavior of business.

First is the basic rationale for businesses to behave properly. Call it the raison d'être for corporate responsibility. Second are efforts to build the skills and intent of the next generation of leaders by encouraging business and other schools to teach corporate and civic responsibility and business ethics as a core component of business or other educational curriculum. Last is the role played by government, civil society, and business associations in efforts to encourage, reward, and incentivize good behavior, and/or discourage bad behavior.

Let's begin with the rationale for proper behavior. In a 1915 manual for successful storekeeping, W. R. Hotchkiss said, "Playing people for suckers is very poor business, and dishonest advertising is the most expensive policy that foolish store keeping permits." He ended his manual with "honesty is the best policy." Less than a decade later, Elbert Gary, the chairman of the board of the world's very first billion-dollar company, U.S. Steel, had an opportunity to speak at his alma mater, Northwestern University. In his remarks, made in 1922, Gary focused on strong business ethics, saying the following:

> There is another convincing reason for . . . the adoption of ethics in business. Sooner or later it pays in dollars and cents. Any man or concern that firmly establishes a reputation for honesty and fair dealing has a business asset of great value and profit.

These speeches and writings were not out of the ordinary 100 years ago. Some believed that ethical behavior was good for business. Others believed it was a moral imperative. Still others believed that to do anything other than behave ethically was counter to religious teachings. Some chose to speak out about the importance of corporate responsibility, while others wrote about it. Without question it influenced some behavior, and while a good deal of those views survive today, it was hardly a strategic or systemic effort.

A Rotary publication (*The Rotarian*) in 1928 published an article titled "The Cash Value of Ethics." It summed up the messaging of a host of trade associations, local and national chambers of commerce, and others, and attempted to influence business action by making the strong case that corporate responsibility and a high level of ethics in the way businesses are run are fundamentally good business.

It was and is critically important to model business behavior after those principles. It was and is also important to identify potential negative results of behaving poorly, such as losing market share, negatively affecting brand value, or risking government sanctions and interference.

While many companies embraced this view, many more did not. Milton Friedman, a renowned economist who served in the Nixon administration, came close to disavowing it by saying, "There is one and only one social responsibility of business, to use its resources and energies in activities designed to increase its profits as long as it stays within the rules of the game, which is to say, engages in open and free competition without deceit or fraud." Were companies to follow that edict they might have gotten the message and chosen not to engage in corporate philanthropy; they also might not have supported paid vacations, overtime, and employer-provided health insurance, and most certainly would not have adopted codes of conduct for their supply chains. However, if we use the data that we now have access to, it is clear from its review that corporate responsibility does equate to the bottom line. It adds to the bottom line.

Can Ethics Be Taught?

The second strategy is to address the need for ethical behavior via business ethics education in business schools and business courses. A number of business schools have led the way, such as Harvard, Stanford, Wharton, and Northwestern, by developing curriculum and coursework on business ethics. While such courses never became a requirement for an MBA, they were increasingly popular and were taught by most business schools in the middle and latter part of the twentieth century.

The establishment of business schools and the academic discipline of teaching the skills required to be successful in business began in the mid-nineteenth century, first at Tulane University in New Orleans, in Louisiana. As the nineteenth century ended and the twentieth century began, there was a proliferation of business schools and programs. Of course, at that time, like today, many business leaders had no formal business academic training, and many others believed that success in business had little to nothing to do with academic skills. Nevertheless, as business schools developed, the focus on business ethics and business behavior developed as well.

The American Association of Collegiate Schools of Business did a study of business schools in 1925–26, including a survey of over two hundred key leaders at those schools. The survey showed that 85 percent of respondents believed that introducing a social point of view into business was an appropriate aim. Yet despite this view, business schools came late to the concept of actually including courses in business ethics, and if they did, it was virtually always a single stand-alone, optional course. In this same study, business school leaders were also asked how many hours of study were devoted to business and the public, a broad euphemism for anything resembling corporate engagement or involvement in society, and the results showed that only 3,800 hours of study were allocated for it, compared with 22,000 hours for accounting, over 17,000 hours for banking and finance, and more than 16,000 hours for economics. Only 287 hours were devoted to teaching business ethics.

By the mid-1980s, there were approximately 500 business ethics courses taught to 40,000 students annually, with more than 20 textbooks on the topic. And yet the notion that ethics should be more than a stand-alone course but part of how one would teach or learn finance, marketing, human resources, or any other core business course was not even on the agenda. By the middle of the twentieth century there was some real progress with a significant increase in the number of schools teaching business ethics, with some even modeling behavior in their own activities or launching a focus on corporate responsibility via separate institutes. But still the idea of integrating ethics into the broader business school curriculum, whether marketing or finance, was not on the agenda. And it is not only schools of business that need to stress ethics. Medical ethics began to be taught in the 1960s, but as with business schools as a stand-alone course. There are of course courses in public policy schools, law schools, medical schools, and other academic disciplines that teach ethics as it relates to specific professional training, but it is not part of how individuals are educated across subjects in every discipline. And ethics are not part of how education is delivered at the elementary and secondary levels on a system-wide basis either.

With respect to government, businesses and business associations, and civil society encouraging or rewarding ethical business behavior, the track record is mixed at best here too. In civil society or not-for-profit enterprises, business leaders have created nonprofit organizations, served on their boards of directors or as trustees of such organizations, and been intimately involved in their scalability and sustainability. While it has been common practice for such organizations to bestow honors upon business leaders as a fund-raising strategy, civil society in a historical context has played a limited role in either recognizing or rewarding business or business leaders' exemplary ethical practice, board service, or anything beyond the standard tax deductions for financial contributions. Government has played an even less significant role. There have been some examples of business leaders who have successfully transitioned from business positions into government or not-for-profit leadership, and examples of individuals who have made the transition from government into business or not-for-profit enterprise, but not many.

Most companies have a set of corporate values, ethics, or principles like Johnson & Johnson's credo. There appear to be a set of common elements of such core principles: accountability, balance, commitment, community, diversity, empowerment, integrity, ownership, and safety. They are adapted to meet individual corporate values and ethics. For example, at American Express they include things like customer satisfaction, quality, integrity, teamwork, respect for people, good citizenship, and personal accountability. While some of the values around community or citizenship are clearly connected to societal values, it is hard to have a value or principle about respect or integrity while simultaneously engaging in bad business practices that would conflict with those kinds of values. The challenge for companies is to combine values with employee engagement. And to make sure all are connected to core elements of the company, from performance to compensation.

Failure on all of these levels has basically left it to individual business leaders to exhibit their leadership, and for government to step in to either regulate or deregulate based on the winds of change, largely influenced by how often negative examples or greed and bad behavior break through in the media.

But is business behavior, both the positive and the negative, unique to business? Is there something about the profit motive, commercialism, or competitiveness that encourages bad behavior in business more than any other sector of the economy? Once again, a review of history will show that this is not the case. Since its inception, American government at the federal, state, and local levels is filled with examples of positive and negative behavior by elected officials. Some American presidents, governors, mayors, and legislators are iconic for accomplishing unbelievably great things. Starting with the Founding Fathers through Lincoln to both Roosevelts and into the modern era, we know the successes. But we also know the scandals.

In the 1870s when negative business behavior was a focus due to the robber barons, the Grant administration had the Whiskey Ring, a cadre of government officials who hid a 70-cents-a-gallon whiskey tax and made inappropriate contributions to the president's election campaign. Around the same time, a shell company called Credit Mobilier provided cheap stock to buy the favor of more than a dozen senators and congressmen. In the 1920s, under President Warren G. Harding, a cabinet member took bribes and stole public funds as part of the Teapot Dome scandal. In the 1930s, the Republican governor of North

Dakota, William Langer, pressured his state employees to contribute to his campaign. And the list goes on. Some who were involved were elected, others appointed. Does this mean all public officials are corrupt and disregard the needs of their voters or constituents? Hardly. Abraham Lincoln signed the Emancipation Proclamation, freed the slaves, and brought the country out of the Civil War; Teddy Roosevelt created the national parks; Franklin Roosevelt got the country though its greatest economic collapse and in his fourth term brought the nation closer to victory in the Second World War. There are many examples of leadership at the state and local levels as well, and some programs championed by public officials have obtained broad bipartisan support, like Social Security and the Peace Corps. High standards of behavior among public officials are essential to building the public's trust in government. And yet there will always be those who betray the public's trust. But government behavior is not universally good or bad. Believing that government is always wrong or always inefficient or always corrupt leads one down the wrong path.

The not-for-profit world is no less culpable. There is the example of the head of the United Way, who in 1995 was jailed for diverting $1.2 million in funds donated for charitable purposes and using them to enrich himself. The Foundation for New Era Philanthropy was essentially a Ponzi scheme and helped nobody in any way. The daughter of the founder of Hale House in New York, which did great work creating a community social safety net, used nearly half a million dollars donated for charity to buy a personal art collection. The president of the Cancer Fund for America diverted funds for personal use. Standards of behavior in the not-for-profit arena have focused on the percentage of agency budgets spent on administration versus direct service, and while important, it is not nearly as important as a broader commitment to strong ethical practice. And that list goes on as well. Does that mean those involved in charitable endeavors are corrupt? Hardly.

The American settlement house community, long before government at any level played any role, resettled refugees and provided needed services to communities across the United States. It was those settlement houses that defined mental health services, creating the model that became the federal Head Start program and other components of the social safety net. Safe Horizons is the largest network of services for abused and neglected women in the United States, and while it is supported by government and private funding, it is an independent not-for-profit organization. The American Cancer Society provides lifesaving and life-changing services to those fighting the disease. It is difficult to image any geography getting through a natural or man-made disaster without the assistance of the Red Cross or dealing with refugee crises without the International Rescue Committee. Each of these not-for-profit organizations exists with the support of business leaders and philanthropic support from businesses as well. Their behavior and very existence are examples of commitment to society and solving societal problems, but there have always been those in that sector who have abused the public trust, and likely that will always be the case. However, we are wise enough not to blame the entire sector for the sins of the few.

In the case of charities and government, we have clearly seen the same chronology—ample examples of abuse juxtaposed against very positive examples of true leadership. In response to behavior good and bad, there are examples of regulation and legislation designed to address problems or support progress in each sector. And, just like in the private sector, some have succeeded and some have not. Has there been a systemic way to take the examples of success in any of the three sectors to scale, and make them the rule not the exception? And, importantly, to understand and reflect the fact that each sector depends on the others? The answer is, not yet. And perhaps most important is to recognize and acknowledge that each sector—government, private, not-for-profit—has influence and effect on the others, both positive and negative. Business has and can play a role in working effectively with the public sector. Or when business leader transition to public service and leverage their skills, talent, and networks to make a difference, they can be a model for others.

The Recent Past

In the latter half of the twentieth century we witnessed a change in how companies approached corporate responsibility. In the 1970s, there was a voluntary effort for corporations to increase their corporate philanthropic contributions. Some committed to philanthropic commitments at 2 percent of net earnings before taxes. There was a parallel movement in the same period to expand matching grants, so employees could have contributions to their alma mater or favored charities matched by their employers. Some companies also matched the volunteer time contributed by their employees as well. In the 1980s and '90s, corporate responsibility reporting became more common, and went beyond philanthropy to include reporting on environmental, labor, and supply chain practices. Of course, that does not mean that everyone agreed that enhanced focus and action by business was an essential goal. Milton Friedman got an enormous amount of attention for deriding corporate responsibility, famously saying that businesses ought to "make as much money as possible" and that the only entities responsible for anything are individuals. To him, companies didn't have any social responsibility of any kind. Of course, today there is evidence that shows that strong corporate responsibility practices can directly equate to financial returns, adding a bit of nuance to Mr. Friedman's quotes. There was also a focus near the end of the twentieth century on corporate governance practices. And while many companies moved to the head of the pack as exemplars of good behavior, it did not prevent high-profile examples of bad behavior to persist, such as Enron, WorldCom, and others. Clearly if we are to move forward in a more effective way, we need to examine further what was done in the past and what we are doing now to fashion policies and practices, across sectors, that move us beyond some good and some not-so-good players.

If the goal is to create a more effective way to involve business in society, connect it effectively to societal needs, and work collaboratively with civil society, history and the facts can clearly teach us a lot. The facts, not just the rhetoric, are enough to disprove the notion that the criticism of business or any sector is universal. The examples of the past can and should inform us about what not to do right now, but are critical as well in helping us to fashion solutions for the future.

We must first examine the degree to which the business sector believes that sound and effective corporate responsibility affects their bottom line. Here we can look to a vitally important study conducted by Robert Eccles and Ioannis Ioannou titled "The Impact of Corporate Sustainability on Organizational Processes and Performance." For a period of nearly 20 years beginning in the early 1990s, they examined 180 companies, reviewing their stock performance along with accounting performance. Their findings demonstrate that those companies that voluntarily adopted a range of forward-thinking sustainability practices significantly outperformed companies that did not. The high-performing companies, many of them profiled in this book, integrated sustainability into their business model, and the low performers did not. Their examination is particularly significant because they did not compare apples to oranges, but instead looked sector by sector, very different from a lot of other corporate social responsibility comparisons. The average assets of the companies examined were over $8 billion. In addition to environmental reporting, the authors looked at labor practices, human rights, stakeholder engagement, and a number of other complex issues including the quality of reporting and the comparability year to year, sector to sector, and company by company to avoid error. Of the high-performing companies, 25 percent of them integrated their social impact into their business strategies and 32 percent integrated their environmental actions and reporting. Among low performers the numbers are starkly different, 5 percent and 10 percent, respectively. The most important finding is in examining the impact on the bottom line. Were an investor to have invested $1 in the high performers, over the 20-year period this would have resulted in a $25 return on investment. Had an investor put $1 into one of the low performers over the same period, they would have had a return of $15. The case is clear: high performance in corporate responsibility has a decidedly positive effect on the bottom line. And more important, this analysis does not even tell the whole story.

Second, we must look at the degree to which businesses mitigate risk and maximize reward via their corporate responsibility behavior. On the risk side, will a company see the value of its brand decrease as a consequence of its failure to address these issues? Then there is the degree to which there is a commitment to business ethics throughout the company, reinforced by a set of core values and standards of behavior. Trust is something important to the company brand, but it is also an important internal criterion for establishing excellence. Once these are established, perhaps most important is how they can then be wedded together effectively in a coordinated strategy and sustained over time to create the tools to be able to engage more broadly, moving business leadership forward to new levels of collaboration and partnership with other sectors of the economy. Some companies have mandatory training on issues of business ethics and standards of performance, though this is not uniform across any sector of the economy.

And finally, it is clear that strong and effective business leadership from the top is absolutely essential and makes a huge difference. While corporations have different business models, and many have worked hard to eliminate silos and promote change from all angles, history tells us that leadership from the top cannot be emphasized strongly enough.

So what are the lessons we can learn by going back through the history of corporate engagement in society?

History provides us with a number of important lessons. We need to understand them, and then act going forward in ways that demonstrate we understand the lessons and learn not to repeat efforts that fail.

Lesson number one is that bad behavior by business is something that is hardly unique to any one time period, any one type of company, or any one type of endeavor. The robber barons were just that—robbers. Some were engaged in business and finance, others in manufacturing, others in transportation. And the type of behavior they practiced was not restricted to any time period. In fact, it continued into the future. History does in fact repeat itself. Some of those whose practices are an embarrassment to American history were motivated solely by greed. Others coupled their greed with lack of regard for others based on geography, income, race, or ethnicity. They disregarded law and regulation with impunity. They lacked basic ethics. And while horrific practices that violate any sense of ethics or values have been replicated time and time again in business, such activity was not restricted to businesses or business leaders alone. Far from it. Such practices are found not only in business but in government, at all levels and during many time periods, and in civil society as well.

And just like the business examples, the examples of bad behavior by government and civil society were also generally motivated by lack of ethics, fueled by greed and patent disregard for others, advanced to achieve self-aggrandizement. But by the same token a trip through history also reveals consistent and repeated examples of just the opposite. Business leaders and companies who led in the area of corporate responsibility exercised their leadership and in return they saw the benefits in their bottom line. And business is not unique. Whether in government, civil society, or business, there are plentiful examples of strong ethics, strong leadership, and a deep commitment to community. Looking back through this historical lens is instructive, but the issue is what we can learn from this journey through history and how it informs where we are today. The lessons of history can empower us to break the cycle.

This brings us to the present.

Chapter 2

Past Is Prologue, but Today Is What Matters

The United States is one of the richest countries in the world, with a GDP significantly higher than that of Europe, Japan, or China, productivity continuing to rise, and the stock market at record levels. Profits for U.S. companies between 2010 and 2014 have grown exponentially, and after-tax profits of U.S. firms as a share of national income exceeded 10.1 percent in 2016, a level last reached right before the Great Depression began in 1929.

Even so, America today, even with the benefits accorded the private sector via the tax system, is still faced with significant economic challenges. While wealth has increased, wages have not. The share of national income paid to U.S. workers has fallen by nearly 8 percent since 1970. And while wages have declined, the decline is far from equal. Higher-income workers receive a growing share of total wages, as the shares of the low- and middle-income segments of the workforce has either been stagnant or has fallen. From 2005 through 2014, income from wages and capital for eight out of ten U.S. households was either stagnant or declined. With no resolution in sight, it appears that income inequality will continue to increase.

And technological changes, if managed properly, can lead to economic growth and expansion of wages, yet they also run the risk that they will not benefit all Americans or all segments of the economy. This has led to political challenges across the United States, along with a good deal of scapegoating. Americans' views of the public sector are hardly positive. Public opinions of Congress are negative, and polls show that some of that bad feeling translates down to states and localities as well. The private sector is also subject to negative sentiments, and changes in public attitudes toward the private sector are not something that ought to be taken lightly. The stock market soars; corporate profits rise; wages and income for the top 1 percent increase; and the gap between senior executives and employees grows. But at the same time, those in the middle and at the bottom face an increasingly uncertain future.

While this is not the first time that America has had to deal with serious economic challenges and inequity between the "haves" and "have-nots," the causes are complex, and blame, to the extent that placing blame is productive, can be shared across all sectors of the economy. While the data and the facts are undeniable, and examples of corporate bad behavior—whether Bernie Madoff and his $65 billion Ponzi legacy or the bogus accounts set up by employees of Wells Fargo—are still very much in the public consciousness, the solutions have been tough to outline and even tougher to implement. Thus, the number of Americans who place blame on all companies continues to rise exponentially.

At the same time, at least in some quarters, the corporate responsibility of today has gone through a significant transformation. In fact, higher standards have been established for corporate conduct. Corporate responsibility reporting is more the rule than the exception, and standards for such reporting have been increased and are more diverse. Independent rating entities—and there are literally hundreds of them—have proliferated and established a range of explicit standards applied to corporate behaviors. In years past, such standards and reporting tended to focus in the main on the extent of a company's philanthropy, diversity, and strong environmental practices. Now they are much more comprehensive and include corporate governance, labor practices, supply chain practices, employee volunteerism, community engagement, and a range of other issues. But while this is all to the good, there are weaknesses, too. Despite being more comprehensive, the standards seldom focus on the entire company and its total business practices and business strategy. While outcomes are assessed in some areas, in far too many, they are not. Importantly, they far too infrequently connect to major and critical societal issues in significant ways.

A range of organizations in the not-for-profit sector regularly review corporate performance against those standards, and the results are often made public and considered by socially responsible investors, advocacy organizations, sometimes by government, and very often by the media. Private consulting entities, universities, and even the not-for-profit entities engaged in the rating and review process have established themselves as consultants and advisors to assist companies in their effort to comply, raise their performance, and ultimately achieve recognition for good behavior. This has gone far beyond a U.S. activity; it involves global companies, globally situated not-for-profits, and others. All this activity has definitely led to improved awareness and improved performance by some companies, causing many to raise the significance and importance of their corporate responsibility function, increase their budgets, raise the level of reporting structures, and create the semblance of an actual profession in the field of corporate responsibility, including certain professional credentials. It has also led to the expansion of executive education and other internal skill-building efforts, an increased focus within business schools, and external recognition programs.

In fact, there are now over 100 different rating and ranking systems that examine private-sector performance. Not all the ratings make sense. Some look at corporate governance and, for example, might give positive credits and points to a company if its board members serve on no more than two corporate boards (based on the view that by serving on more boards the individual would have less time to devote to his or her board duties). And yet the same standard applies to current CEOs as it does to retired CEOs. Might someone who is retired have time to serve on more boards of directors than someone who is a current CEO? Of course. Should the standard be more closely aligned with actual practice? Of course. In other ratings, a company's positive financial performance is counted as a corporate responsibility positive characteristic. Shouldn't a company be rewarded, not penalized, if its corporate responsibility was exemplary in spite of a financial downturn? Of course. Another asks companies to adopt a policy on human rights, and those that do get favorable points. However, this has nothing to do with actually implementing such a policy or spreading it across your industry or supply chain. Should those who have adopted a human rights policy also be held accountable for implementing it? Of course. In an area like corporate philanthropy, the grades are high for the level of funding, and have precious little to do with the results or benefits of such funding. Should company actions focus on genuine outcomes? Of course. With regard to environmental performance, the same standards are applied to companies regardless of their line of business, with strong environmental performance by a consulting or financial services company juxtaposed against an advanced manufacturer or oil and gas company. Shouldn't environmental performance connect to the actual line of business of the company? Of course. In virtually every other area of private-sector operations, metrics are what drives performance. This ought to be the case with respect to corporate responsibility as well. Companies must define levels of performance with clear metrics and then offer opportunities based on performance against those metrics. Further, those results should be made available to the public.

Clearly a good deal more needs to be done in refining the standards of behavior linked to ratings, but obviously some ratings are worthwhile and can instigate change. As just one example, in the late 2000s, Coca-Cola saw its ratings drop on the Broad Market Social Index as a result of some less than positive activities on labor issues in the developing world. As a direct result, TIAA-CREF sold 50 million shares of Coca-Cola stock, which then led the company to make a variety of very positive changes in its labor relations, resulting in a rebound of its index ratings. Subsequently the company has put a major focus on clean water in the developing world to display not just its reactive means of addressing social issues, but to show that it is addressing these issues in a proactive fashion.

While the corporate responsibility bar has been raised, and will likely continue to be, it has not totally affected instances of bad behavior by some companies, which still continue into the twenty-first century. In fact, some companies with strong ratings and high corporate responsibility status on independent rating schemes have been found to engage in bad ethics and bad corporate practices concurrent with such formal recognition for their excellence in corporate responsibility. Shortly before the Volkswagen scandal emerged, in which the company had fraudulently hidden its efforts to evade fuel standards and was ultimately convicted of malfeasance, *Forbes* magazine ranked Volkswagen as one of the top ten companies for corporate social responsibility. This is reminiscent of Enron, which was honored by the Environmental Protection Agency and was presented with a major award for its corporate social responsibility achievements by the Council on Economic Priorities right before the incidence of fraud and abuse surfaced. Enron was disgraced, its leaders imprisoned, and the company went out of business. There are many other examples as well. But is this any different from the errors made by financial analysts whose ratings of the financial performance of a company inaccurately provided a positive view, only to see the company's stock plummet or company auditors like Arthur Andersen hiding questionable financial practices?

While overall a good deal of positive change has taken place, it has not positively affected public attitudes about corporations. In fact, the reverse is true, to the point where the public, instead of understanding the result as a range of cross-sector activities, lays the blame for problems like income inequality, educational quality and access, and environmental issues squarely at the feet of the private sector, the billionaire class, and the behavior of Wall Street firms. Some would argue that the egregious behavior by felons like Bernie Madoff or bad practices by Wells Fargo and Volkswagen, which both companies have moved to rectify, counts for a good deal more, affecting public attitudes much more than the professionalization of rating schemes, corporate responsibility awards, or positive and meaningful behaviors that have benefited society.

The same is true of other positive developments. Corporate philanthropy continues to increase; employer-sponsored volunteerism has increased as well. More companies comply with Global Reporting Initiative standards of behavior, and more produce corporate responsibility reports. Most of the nation's top business schools teach courses in corporate social responsibility or business ethics, and some, like Harvard, Stanford, and the Northwestern Kellogg School of Management, have made them integral to their curriculum. There are also numerous examples of corporations speaking out publicly on key issues that clearly involve business but also have deep connections to societal issues. One prime example is how companies have publicly identified themselves with leadership performance on environmental issues. When the Paris climate accord was agreed on in 2015, many companies spoke out in support of climate change as a critical problem, and when the United States announced it would withdraw from the agreement, a host of companies vocally criticized the Trump administration. The same is true of diversity issues. After the violence sparked by the rally of white supremacists in Charlottesville, Virginia, in August 2017, many companies chose to speak out. Kenneth Frazier, the CEO of Merck, and other key CEOs felt so strongly about President Trump's rhetoric in response to the events in Charlottesville that Frazier resigned from the president's advisory council on manufacturing, which ultimately led to the members calling for the council to disband. Many companies also voiced their opposition to "bathroom bills" in North Carolina and Texas to preserve the rights of transgender individuals. Companies also publicly identified with the plight of so-called Deferred Action for Childhood Arrivals (DACA), or "Dreamers," supporting the continuation of the policy, and have voiced their strong opposition to broader immigration restrictions. And companies have gone beyond voicing their opposition to the NRA. They have begun to actually cease investing in gun manufacturers.

Companies are responding to pressure from their employees who have been forthright in asking their company leaders to declare their support for policies that are consistent with their broader societal concerns, while other companies react to behavior by consumers or a variety of interest groups that are looking to penalize companies that do not speak out. However, the leadership of many more companies believe that when political or policy decisions, even by the president of the United States, conflict with a company's core beliefs, they must speak out, despite the threats or possible consequences.

The challenge in the current context is threefold: (1) to see whether progress in corporate responsibility and positive behavior by some companies can increase even more and much more rapidly; (2) whether bad corporate behavior can be curtailed significantly; and (3) whether public attitudes can help spur positive actions across all sectors of the economy. Most important, we need to determine whether such activities can be sustainable and scalable, producing significant, measurable business and societal results.

This allows us to go beyond simply checking a box, such as a human rights policy or a corporate responsibility report, and transcend a simplistic set of criteria, which ought to be met at a minimum. Instead we rise to the next level: identify a critical societal issue, and connect to actual impact and results. This could be something on the level of stepping up and creating the management system for Social Security (as IBM did in 1937), or establishing a new employee benefit, as was the case with paid vacations, health insurance, pensions (as American Express did in 1875), paid family leave, and tuition reimbursement, or critical policy issues like education or global health. And not to stop there, but to take the next step to ensure that the effort is scalable and sustainable over a respectable period of time. Rosabeth Moss Kanter, professor at the Harvard Business School, refers to this as "going from spare change to real change"—spare change being the donation of excess profits, and real change being contributing the best that a company has to offer in a substantive fashion to address deeply intractable societal challenges.

There are some very concrete examples through which we can drive home this point.

Best Practices in Corporate Responsibility

In the past, a company's labor practices were critically important in identifying its ethics and behavior. This translated into a focus on higher wages, limits on hours of work per week, better working conditions, paid vacation, pensions, and health insurance. Today those practices include recognition of same-sex marriage and domestic partner benefits, paid family leave, expanded training and education services, and support for elder care along with the more traditional benefits. Perhaps most significant for global companies is their insistence that they and their suppliers engage in practices that mirror positive corporate practices. Environmental performance and a commitment to sustainability have been important for some time, especially for manufacturers, but these priorities have been expanded to include recycling in company cafeterias, encouragement of energy-saving practices by employees, and political support for efforts to slow climate change.

While companies have long valued corporate philanthropy, these efforts have been augmented as well through community support and employee volunteerism via matching grants programs, employee charitable campaigns, creation and support of corporate foundations, and time off for community service, which in some cases includes a range of incentives, financial and otherwise, for employees to sustain these service activities.

As significant as these activities are, not many companies have standards of behavior or activity that focus on actual results, including metrics for performance. Fewer still engage in collaborative activities with other companies, with government, or with other public or nonprofit organizations in a large-scale collaborative fashion, including measurement of actual results. Government action has focused on behaviors, rather than on providing incentives for higher and higher levels of performance year by year. Among not-for-profit organizations, financial support from companies has been much sought after, for obvious reasons, but far too often checkbook philanthropy has been a key to receiving formal recognition from such organizations for high performance, as opposed to actually delivering higher performance.

It is common practice for not-for-profit organizations seeking financial support for fund-raising dinners to select an honoree for the size of his or her wallet and their ability to generate added financial support from others, as opposed to their actual accomplishments.

As with most problems, we learn the most from examples both positive and negative, along with deep subject knowledge of the problem, an understanding of what success looks like, knowledge of what barriers to higher-quality performance exist and how to overcome them, and perhaps most important, how to rein in poor performance and go from islands of excellence to scalable and sustainable activities.

In order to understand where to go next, let's review some of the most effective examples of recent corporate responsibility. I will do so by examining what problem was addressed, how it was addressed, what results and metrics were established to assess those results, and how the efforts was able to sustain itself. I will then extrapolate key learning from those examples that will allow us to go from the present to the future in a radically improved way. I will also attempt to get behind the facts and tell the personal stories of those involved so they can be truly instructive.

Corporate Responsibility and Education

There is perhaps no societal issue more important than education. A solid education equates directly to success in the private sector and more broadly to a sound economic future. No private company can achieve success without the ability to recruit and retain top talent.

Historically, companies have addressed education in a host of ways but have focused most heavily on higher education. Many companies provide financial support to higher education institutions via student scholarships, faculty support through endowed professorships, and institutional support. Perhaps most significantly, companies offer matching grants where their employees and retirees can make contributions to their alma maters and have them matched with a corporate contribution. While some companies have opened their matching grants up to K–12 institutions, the distribution of such grants is heavily weighted toward higher education.

Some companies have engaged in joint research efforts with higher education. In some instances that support became even more transformative. As discussed in the previous chapter, IBM helped institutions create the academic discipline of computer science. More recently, IBM has been at the forefront in formulating academic programs in nanoscience, data analytics, and artificial intelligence. Other companies have led similar efforts.

While this type of support is valued by and valuable to educational institutions, it has also proven valuable to the corporate donors, assisting them in recruitment of top talent and ensuring that prospective employees complete the academic programs of most relevance to a specific company or industry. However, because support often begins with a connection to the institution via hiring needs or employee or executive connections, an examination of the beneficiaries of such support reveals that the overwhelming majority of it goes to private, not public, institutions and to four-year, not two-year, schools.

It is the public colleges, especially the two-year schools, that serve a disproportionate share of low-income students, especially those of color. There are of course exceptions when we speak of private colleges, especially with respect to support of some historically black colleges and universities, but overall it is clear that those students who benefit the most from corporate support are those from the middle and upper classes, and those who benefit the least are those from the lower and working classes.

While the overall responsibility for performance falls mainly on public education systems themselves, the lack of private-sector support for two-year programs, contrasted with efforts on behalf of four-year schools, certainly contributes to the reality that our higher education system is not one system but two, consisting of haves and have-nots. This problem is exacerbated by the fact that the public does not view the quality of higher education as a significant societal issue. Public concern lies primarily with elementary and secondary education, which is an even more inequitable system of haves and have-nots. Despite this, private support for elementary and secondary education has been less strategic and, despite some successes, overall not very effective.

In total, private support for elementary and secondary public education, coming not just from corporations but from private sources, including private, community, and family foundations, amounts to less than 1 percent of total public-sector spending on K–12 education. In the main, such support has focused on peripheral issues, such as "adopt a school" programs, which were popular and prevalent in the 1990s and translated into donations of books and musical and athletic equipment, and volunteer events. More recently, the highly politicized reaction to the implementation of Common Core education standards in 2009 resulted in many in the private sector avoiding any engagement or involvement in education reform at all. A good deal of support bypassed public schools and went toward charter schools or alternative programs, which while often beneficial for specific schools, has been less systemic and has had less ability to scale. Philanthropic support has also increased in some cases, with philanthropic donations tied to efforts by school districts to institute stronger teacher evaluation systems linked to test results, pay for performance, and other activities that have some positive goals but were also designed to weaken teachers' unions.

The Background on School Reform

If the core problems of education are to be effectively addressed, the private sector must play a more proactive, deliberate, and systemic public role on both a programmatic and policy level. The private sector has a tremendous stake in doing so: the success of elementary and secondary schooling is directly connected to the economic future of companies of all sizes and sectors, as well as the nation.

In the last 10 years, spurred on by a national focus, high school graduation rates have increased markedly across the United States. This is excellent news, but it is not the full story. Currently, only 9 percent of low-income 24-year-olds in the United States have a postsecondary degree, and that has only inched up by 3 percentage points in the last half century. This has taken place at a time when workplace demands have radically changed. From 2007 to 2017, approximately 10 million new U.S. jobs have been created, 99 percent of which require a postsecondary degree. At the same time, approximately 7 million jobs requiring a high school diploma disappeared, with few returning. Jobs requiring postsecondary degrees require higher skill levels and offer higher wages, while those requiring only a high school diploma are largely lower-skill and lower-wage.

Among low-income high school graduates who register at both two- and four-year colleges, a disturbingly low percentage complete their degree, demonstrating that a high school diploma simply does not equate to college readiness. In fact, of low-income high school graduates who register in two-year community colleges, only 6 percent complete their degree on time. Over a three-year period, the number climbs only to about 10 percent, and over six years, only about 20 percent receive a degree. Clearly college readiness and college completion are problems of epic proportions, requiring a comprehensive and shared set of actions involving government at all levels.

Clear evidence of the lack of college readiness is the significantly high level of spending on remedial courses. Despite having earned their high school diploma, far too many students enter college unable to take credit-bearing coursework, and are placed in noncredit remedial courses to build their academic skills. For these students, college can take longer and be more expensive. Such courses proliferate across our higher education system, costing nearly $3 billion a year. Overwhelmingly, remedial courses are taken by low-income students, especially those of color, with dismal success rates. Left unaddressed, these outcomes will impede economic growth, force jobs overseas, and create demands for social services and income supports that will result in the diversion of funding from education, infrastructure, and innovation. This clearly makes the case for action, and swift action to be sure. Such actions can be most effective if they have the full support and engagement of the private sector.

One recent well-meaning effort to engage in elementary and secondary education focused on students at the bottom of the income pyramid in Newark, New Jersey. It was spearheaded and funded by Facebook founder Mark Zuckerberg. While much has been written about the work, perhaps most important was a book by Dale Russakoff called *The Prize*. Russakoff's book reveals that this effort relied less on the involvement of Facebook the company, and more on the personal philanthropy of Mr. Zuckerberg. Thus, the lessons of the engagement and investment are more about philanthropy than about private-sector engagement.

Newark is a city with a serious education crisis—extremely low achievement levels and high dropout rates—contrasted against high per-pupil expenditures. Zuckerberg made a very substantial philanthropic grant of $100 million, insisting upon $100 million in matching funding, which was easily secured. The $200 million total was then focused on a range of investments, including a new teacher evaluation system based on student performance, extensive use of consultants, and the use of significant amounts of private funding to obtain support of key stakeholders. The effort had the support of then Newark mayor (and now senator) Cory Booker and then governor Chris Christie. According to Russakoff's analysis, money alone in K–12 will not solve critical problems. What is required is deep subject-matter knowledge of the issue by the donor, forming the basis for an informed and strategic operational strategy. The barriers to education reform are considerable and must be thoroughly understood before a strategy is put in place to address and remove them.

Of course, the lack of success in this effort is not unique. A decade and a half earlier, in 1993, the Annenberg Foundation, endowed by Walter Annenberg, made a gift of $387 million over five years via the Annenberg Challenge to stimulate large-scale reform across multiple school districts. Annenberg's gift was solely cash and involved none of his business interests. Like Zuckerberg, Annenberg was very successful in business, leading a publishing empire that included *TV Guide*, *Seventeen* magazine, and the *Philadelphia Inquirer*. His influence was broad; he was a very large donor to President Reagan, who eventually appointed him ambassador to Great Britain. As owner of the *Philadelphia Inquirer*, that city's major newspaper, he successfully fought against a gubernatorial candidate who opposed a railroad merger between the Pennsylvania Railroad and the New York Central (Annenberg was the largest shareholder in the Pennsylvania Railroad). However, despite its deep pockets and some experience augmented by access to some exemplary educators, the Annenberg educational effort proved largely unsuccessful. An August 2003 final technical report of the Chicago Annenberg Research Project by the Consortium on Chicago School Research said that while "student achievement improved across Annenberg Challenge schools as it did across the Chicago Public School system as a whole, results suggest that among the schools it supported, the Challenge had little impact on school improvement and student outcomes, with no statistically significant differences between Annenberg and non-Annenberg schools in rates of achievement gain, classroom behavior, student self-efficacy, and social competence."

Bill Gates, perhaps the world's best-known billionaire and most generous philanthropist, also has attempted to reform schools with cash donations to promote and bring to scale "small schools" that promise a stronger community environment with greater individual attention for students. This too involved philanthropy—the Gates Foundation—not engagement by the Microsoft Corporation. Over five years and approximately $2 billion invested, the results, while successful in some ways, specifically those initiated by New Visions in New York City and some charter schools like KIPP, did not produce the strong outcomes envisioned. Gates, disappointed, chose to focus his efforts elsewhere for a time, and recently launched a new fact-based effort to build upon some of the most promising efforts in school reform where he believes his support can be instrumental, especially involving the connection between school and career. To implement these efforts, he has engaged some very experienced educators.

I should note that my knowledge of these efforts also comes firsthand. I played a role in initiating the small schools movement in New York City that the Gates Foundation ultimately supported, with significant private foundation funding of over $1 billion. As deputy schools chancellor to New York City's then chancellor Joe Fernandez, I attempted, with some success, to bring small schools to scale, going from a few schools that had been in operation for more than a decade, serving small numbers of students in a few geographies, to 30 launched in one year across the city, working initially in partnership with New Visions and other partners. New Visions became a well-regarded entity under the leadership of its chair, Dick Beattie, and its executive directors, first Beth Lief and then Bob Hughes.

Before my role at the New York City Department of Education, I founded a think tank called Interface, where I spearheaded a feasibility study for the New York Community Trust, America's largest community foundation, whose support led to the creation of New Visions. I also convinced both then school chancellor Richard Green and then Board of Education chairman Robert F. Wagner Jr., along with Mayor Ed Koch, to support it, and for over a decade I served on its board. I also had significant involvement with many of the recipients of the Annenberg Challenge in New York City, specifically in the old Community School District 4, led by Tony Alvarado. I thus knew both programs from the inside and have had a fairly close association with several key leaders and consultants who were eventually invited in and engaged with the Newark reform efforts.

From my vantage point, there are numerous lessons we can glean from these significant investments in school reform. Clearly even the most talented business leaders, fueled by genuine interest and willingness to invest hundreds of millions or billions of dollars, can produce results that don't measure up, especially when trying to apply their checkbooks alone against the daunting challenge of achieving lasting school reform. Education over the last several years has become incredibly politicized. It appears as if there is no issue in education that is not divisive.

Take the matter of academic standards. Higher academic standards enjoyed the bipartisan support of governors, education, and business leaders, especially after the three National Education Summits led by IBM in 1996, 1998, and 2001. Yet as the Common Core national standard rolled out across states in 2009, its support diminished, becoming a target for opposition from both the left and the right. Sadly, the political leaders who had supported higher standards and Common Core read the polling data indicating Common Core's waning popularity and retreated, and so did many private-sector leaders.

I chaired a task force that Governor Andrew Cuomo created on the Common Core implementation in New York, and the only thing key stakeholders could agree on was to delay its implementation. Teacher evaluation, not the standards themselves, unfortunately, became inextricably linked to standards and accountability, and as a result it became another incredibly divisive issue, with strong opposition from the teachers' union and antitesting groups, in contrast to vocal support from many on the right who mischaracterized the Common Core as a federal initiative. With performance levels in America's schools stalled, I, and many others, would have hoped that support for higher standards would have united constituencies and not divided them, much in the way it has united governors across political persuasions at the education summit meetings. Had teacher evaluation not become intertwined with standards, and even more importantly, had educators pursued a "big tent" strategy and engaged parents directly in its rollout, perhaps schools would be achieving against those standards at even higher levels today. Surprisingly, issues that could easily produce unity, such as the need for higher-quality instruction and professional development for teachers and engagement of parents and communities, have been relegated to a backseat. And many in the private sector have joined those in the backseat, feeling that engaging on education reform is a zero-sum game. Of course, this is not in their interest from a business standpoint, or from a corporate responsibility standpoint, and must be reversed.

Charter schools and increased school choice for parents in their children's education is another issue that has become incredibly divisive. New and innovative models of education and learning should not be resisted, but rather embraced. It is not whether, but how, such innovation is developed and implemented that becomes the potential problem. There was a time when the American Federation of Teachers, under Albert Shanker, was a supporter of charter schools and increased school choice. In fact, Shanker believed, as did many others, that the opportunity to design new and effective strategies in such schools, especially with the engagement of teachers, would ultimately lead to those efforts being embraced and mainstreamed in all schools. Sadly, that did not turn out to be the case. And while some charter schools clearly are very effective, others are not. And most disappointing, the most effective strategies used have seldom found their way into mainstream efforts in public schools as was initially envisioned. Just like the push on academic standards, this too can be given a fresh look and a different implementation strategy.

Reforms in education are difficult but certainly not impossible. Successful strategies take time, beginning with a deep understanding of the subject, including knowledge of the operational, policy, and especially the political issues involved in making change. This must be coupled with evidence-based hypotheses of what potential innovation can achieve and the financial and social costs of that innovation. If change is stimulated by outside forces, whether via private foundations or corporations, they must be inclusive of the experts on the ground—implemented through public-private partnerships with key stakeholders in the education system. This is not a legal partnership effort but a deep collaboration where a common goal and strategy is adopted and implemented. Critically important is to understand and capitalize on the pressure that can be applied by certain key stakeholders, who represent teachers, principals, parents, and communities, and to have a firm grounding in the financial interests and governance issues involving states and localities, as well as the federal government. Innovations also must include long-term goals and metrics for success; outcomes data must be reviewed, publicly shared, and used as a basis for ongoing improvement; and finally, all meaningful changes must include a strategy to scale and make it sustainable. All of this needs to be addressed concurrently, not sequentially, in order to be effective.

There are a host of added ways the private sector can assist in school reform efforts. Helping to smooth the transition from school to college to career is clearly one. Supporting necessary policy changes is another, whether improving standards and accountability or supporting fair and more effective funding models. But through closer cooperation and coordination there will be further opportunities to plan and then execute efforts that benefit society.

Let's examine a couple of existing initiatives designed to address the issue of education reform in a meaningful and collaborative way to see what we can learn, not just about what to do and what not to do, but how to do it in a way that achieves significant results and holds the promise of expansion and scale for all students.

P-TECH: Reinventing High Schools

It was with a deep knowledge of what works and what doesn't that IBM began an effort to reform high school education via the P-TECH 9–12 School Model. This was certainly not the first time in U.S. history that high school was reimagined. At the end of the Second World War, America began an effort to make high school attendance mandatory. Before that, the nation essentially had a K–12 system of education, where completion of grade eight was mandatory and high school was optional. As states began to shift education policy and make high school mandatory, largely as an economic necessity, some companies supported that effort, IBM included. The leadership to make this switch, however, came largely from the political and education arena rather than the private sector. A major change in college attendance was also instituted at that time via passage of the GI Bill, and while that had private-sector support from companies like IBM, it also was led by government and political forces.

As discussed in the previous chapter, IBM was hardly a newcomer to education reform. Under the leadership of chairman and CEO Lou Gerstner, IBM led the nation's governors and CEOs, along with the president of the United States, through three National Education Summits. The genesis of the summits began with Gerstner's speech before the National Governors Association's biannual meeting in Vermont in the summer of 1995. He challenged them to act as CEOs of their states and assume responsibility for education improvement. These summits chose to focus laserlike on the issues of standards and accountability, which resulted in the creation of such systems. At the time of the initial summit in 1996, only 13 states had established education standards; by 1999, virtually all states had developed academic standards. The summit in 1996 also launched Achieve, which Gerstner chaired and which stands to this day as one of the most effective not-for-profit organizations effectuating education reform.

Also in 1996, IBM initiated its Reinventing Education program to assist states, districts, and international ministries of education to implement education change strategies. In 1998, IBM created the KidSmart Early Learning Program, which centered on a child-friendly and collaborative computer learning station that provided millions of young children around the world with access to specially designed hardware and software solutions along with teacher training. It was favorably assessed in a report prepared for the European Union. IBM also created two innovative software tools using automatic language translation and voice recognition, which has been successful in helping millions of low-performing students improve their literacy skills. Over more than a decade, these innovations produced significant successes at the school, district, state, and national levels. Some were sustained over more than a decade. Notably, they did not just involve philanthropy. Rather, they engaged the company's best technology solutions and began in the IBM research centers, involving both hardware and software engineers, along with the volunteer time of its employees and the problem-solving capabilities of some of its most talented researchers and consultants. IBM was only half the equation; in every instance, we partnered with educators to inform and guide our work. In that period, other companies were active as well. American Express exerted leadership in helping advance the academy movement and the creation of the National Academy Foundation that has created a network of grades 9–12 high schools with a theme connected to businesses.

The idea of P-TECH was sparked in 2010, at the U.S. Open Tennis Championship in Flushing Meadows Corona Park, New York. IBM's then CEO, Sam Palmisano, and then chancellor of schools, Joel Klein, sat together as they had done many times before. Instead of reliving how closely they had worked together when Klein was at the White House working for then president Bill Clinton and Palmisano offered his expertise on the information technology industry, they began discussing a critical problem identified by Klein: the lack of connection between high schools and jobs in the city.

In 2010, New York City was beginning its upswing from the economic downturn that began in 2008, and it needed a lift, especially for those at the bottom rung. Klein asked for IBM's help. Palmisano offered up his head of corporate citizenship and corporate affairs—yours truly—to work on the design of something innovative to address the challenge. The next day, at Sam's request, I spoke to Joel and outlined how unusual it would be for a technology innovation company like IBM to engage in the hiring of large numbers of students who were high school graduates. I suggested a collaboration between IBM, the New York City Department of Education, and the City University of New York (CUNY), the city's public higher education system, offering to engage its then chancellor and a longtime friend and colleague, Matthew Goldstein. Matt and I shared a mentor, former CUNY chancellor Al Bowker, under whose aegis free tuition at CUNY was instituted in the 1960s. Joel endorsed my outreach to Matt and urged me to work on this, "the quicker the better." I spoke to Joel, his staff, and Matt several times that day, and that night developed a several-page outline of what an innovative partnership would look like before sending it to Joel's deputy chancellor, Mark Sternberg, who now heads the education philanthropy efforts at the Walton Foundation. With a few comments and tweaks, they sent it along to then New York City mayor Michael Bloomberg to get his support. They did better than we could ever have imagined when that Sunday, the mayor announced the as-yet-unnamed program on national TV. The next morning, I had a call with Sam Palmisano and outlined the needed next steps, and he provided IBM's full support. With the strong support of Mayor Bloomberg and Chancellor Klein, plus IBM's CEO, Sam Palmisano, the next step would be to bring it to fruition.

It was September 2010, and the clock was ticking on launching a new school model in just one year (minus a day!). The model we designed was a true innovation. It called for a departure from the traditional four years of high school and the creation of a new grades 9–14 school model with a clear scope and sequence on integrated high school and college coursework, leading to both a concurrent high school diploma and an associate's degree. To work, the model, at its foundation, required a strong and seamless partnership between the school district, the community college system, and industry. Industry involvement as a full collaborator was a particularly forward-thinking concept, with IBM committing to help ensure that students would graduate career-ready. These commitments included identifying the technical and professional skills required (problem solving, communication, etc.) for entry-level jobs in the IT industry so that they could be integrated directly into the academic curriculum; a workplace curriculum and worksite visits to expose students early on; professional mentors for all students; high-value paid internships; and professional development for teachers. Tuition for college courses would be free. Students would gain admittance through open enrollment, meaning there were no admissions criteria, and importantly, the six-year program would allow students to progress at their own pace, taking college courses as soon as they demonstrated readiness rather than progressing grade by grade with their peers. Thus, a student could complete the dual degrees in less than six years. Most important, any and all students who successfully completed their associate of applied science (AAS) degree (which, based on the IBM skills map and determined by high school and CUNY faculty, was in either computer information systems or electromechanical engineering technology) would then be "first in line" for an interview for any appropriate job at IBM. This was a guarantee of a job interview, and a powerful motivator and a direct link between high school, college, and career. Of course, students with their two-year degree in hand could also gain acceptance to a four-year college for their bachelor's degree and receive two years of credit toward that degree. The choice would be up to the student.

The P-TECH approach would differ markedly from other efforts to engage technology or technology companies in education. The solution was based on a substantive and integrated instructional model, backed up by strong industry engagement, and not based on hardware or software. In the past there were some who thought that simply giving each child access to a computer would result in achievement gains. It did not. In the current environment some also believe that adding software skills via the teaching of coding or other software skills will boost achievement. The reality is that any use of technology, whether lightbulbs, televisions or computer hardware or software, without a comprehensive academic program that engages educators along with strong private-sector engagement and support will likely be ineffective and could accomplish just the opposite of what is needed, namely a resistance to innovation and change.

With a clear understanding of what derailed many education reforms from the outset, we endeavored to devise a plan that would quickly go from one school to several and would engage the support of key stakeholders as we modified and improved the model while in operation. We resisted turning on the spigot and contributing large amounts of cash to the school, since education reforms that are reliant on large cash donations have a built-in barrier to replication. Rather, this new model of high school would have to rise and fall on the standard per capita spending that schools used. We also fought against admissions screening, knowing that that only worked for those perceived as the best or most gifted students, and would lead only to another built-in barrier to replication. This would be a school model that could work for students regardless of their academic level. Finally, we created the model to abide by all the rules set forth in legislation and regulation at both the state and local levels, rather than seeking waivers of regulatory or collective bargaining issues. Doing so, while tempting, would create yet another built-in barrier that could stand in the way of scalability and sustainability.

The city Department of Education quickly determined that the school would be located in one already slated for closure, the Paul Robeson High School, located across from a public housing project, the Albany Houses, on Albany Avenue in Crown Heights, Brooklyn. Of course, starting at Robeson was a challenge, since the community, like all communities, resists school closures. This was especially true of a school named after an icon in the African American community, situated in a predominantly African American neighborhood. In fact, when the Department of Education announced that Robeson would be closed, there was an outcry from elected officials and community leaders. Al Vann, then a member of the New York State Assembly and a longtime civil rights leader and someone I worked with closely during my tenure as deputy schools chancellor, reached out to me when he heard that I was involved somehow in the design of the school that would replace Robeson. I urged him to convene a meeting with community leaders and give us an opportunity to outline the plans and disengage the concept of the new school model from the closure of Robeson. I wanted to make it clear that this new opportunity would be open to all community residents, especially those in the Robeson community. This meeting and Al Vann's personal leadership were critical in deflating the opposition, resulting in broad support by the city, its school and its higher education system, and the local community.

With that foundation, the next steps were to identify a principal, put in place a faculty, and develop a plan to open the doors in September 2011. Knowing how key the right school leader would be to give birth to a movement, I obtained the support of the larger principal community by reaching out to the head of the principals' union, Ernie Logan, whom I knew well when I sat across the bargaining table with the union. Together, we organized a session for about 20 principals at the IBM offices in New York City to discuss the model and get ideas, suggestions, and, most important, buy-in. We got the buy-in from all, but most importantly, we got a principal. Rashid Davis sat in the back of the room. He raised his hand, asked many questions, and offered some helpful comments. Soon afterward, as we considered options, he was our clear choice to lead the school. I invited him to my home for dinner a few weeks later, a regular practice we continued after he assumed leadership at the school, and it was even clearer that we had made the right choice. Rashid's passion was evident and inspiring, and he was already a lauded educator. Perhaps above all, he believed that the model and all the students who would attend this school would succeed.

That night I asked Rashid what his criteria for determining high-quality faculty were. He outlined the usual academic and teaching experiences and then said that he would ask each potential staff member to sign on to the notion that 100 percent of the students would be successful in achieving their high school diploma and associate's degree, and they would see it as their mission to let not even one student fall between the cracks. I literally got goose bumps as I listened.

There were different kinds of bumps along the way, to be sure. Because the school was formalized after the first round of the New York City high school application process was completed, the entire first cohort of students at the school were students who had not obtained any of their top twelve high school choices. This meant that a distinct majority of the students enrolled were not attending based upon a clear and direct interest in being part of a rigorous program focused on IT. On a good note, given our determination to create a model that could work for any student, regardless of their academic performance through eighth grade, no person could accuse the school leadership of creaming the population.

Despite the bumps, the school, now named P-TECH (or Pathways in Technology Early College High School) opened its doors as planned with a little over 100 ninth graders, all of whom were low-income children of color. Before the school opened, we put the word out among IBM employees and were quickly able to recruit a mentor for every student. We also hired a school-based staff person, a former Teach for America teacher in New York, who would be responsible for implementing our commitments, be our eyes and ears at the school day in and day out, and support the principal, faculty, and students. Also, before the school opened, we brought the faculty to IBM for a two-day training and skill-building workshop, and at the end of the 48-hour session we were one cohesive and missioned group. To maintain shared governance over decision making, a school-based steering committee was formed consisting of all the key decision makers from the Department of Education, CUNY, the New York City College of Technology, which was the college within CUNY that would grant the two AAS degrees, and

IBM, led by myself. By midyear, there already were results to celebrate, including high school performance rates and workplace engagements.

When newly elected Chicago mayor Rahm Emanuel came to New York to meet with Mayor Bloomberg to see what he could learn from Bloomberg's leadership in New York, he heard directly from Mayor Bloomberg that P-TECH should be high on his list. When Mayor Emanuel hit the street that December afternoon, he immediately whipped out his cell phone and called IBM's CEO to request that IBM bring the P-TECH innovation to Chicago—but with one change: he wanted five schools, not one (which says a lot about the mayor's competitive nature).

With the Brooklyn school scarcely halfway through its first year, we moved to negotiate P-TECH in Chicago with Mayor Emanuel. He wanted all five schools to open in the fall of 2012, eight months away, and offered a new building on the South Side of Chicago for the school where IBM would serve as the industry collaborator, which was ultimately named after Sarah E. Goode, one of the first African American women to earn a U.S. patent. When we indicated that he needed other companies on board to lead the other schools, he garnered support from Microsoft, Verizon, Motorola, and Cisco and scheduled a press conference within weeks to announce them. Building toward the announcement, however, he had stopped referring to the schools as grades 9–12, instead referring to them as traditional grades 9–12 STEM high schools. This seemed troubling and hardly accidental. However, during the press conference when I had the opportunity to speak right before Mayor Emanuel, I thanked him for his leadership in bringing the P-TECH grades 9–12 model to Chicago and stressed the fact that the program would not be a traditional high school. He didn't flinch, evidenced his strong support, and we were on our way.

Shortly after Sarah E. Goode STEM Academy opened, I had the opportunity to visit the school along with a cadre of hundreds of IBM mentors. In speaking to the group of about 250 ninth graders, I told them that they were in college, not high school, and that IBM as a company was behind them to ensure their success. Shortly thereafter, P-TECH was the subject of a *Time* magazine cover story and a PBS special. This significant attention from the media was instrumental in leading to significant and expanded interest from political and education leaders across the country.

In Chicago, we followed the Brooklyn playbook, with an onsite industry liaison—another person with teaching experience—a principal we had a hand in choosing, and a quickly constructed partnership with Richard J. Daley College, which at that point did not even offer an AAS degree in computer science. The bumps we had in New York were nothing like the bumps we encountered in Chicago. The Chicago Public Schools repeatedly tried to backtrack on commitments, largely due to their lingering financial crisis and strain with the Chicago Teachers Union. But we held our ground and insisted that success needed to be based on what was working in Brooklyn, which, as a result of Rashid Davis and his faculty's leadership, was already showing significant promise. Had we backed down, subsequent replication efforts could have resulted in less and less fidelity to the model, and a promise to children and their families would be broken.

As word of the model spread, the Brooklyn school received numerous visits from key influencers, ranging from the head of the American Federation of Teachers, Randi Weingarten, who I had negotiated contracts with during my tenure as deputy chancellor, to university presidents like Ron Daniels of Johns Hopkins University. Daniels visited P-TECH at the suggestion of Sam Palmisano, who served on the Hopkins board along with Mayor Bloomberg. I took him into Jamilah Seifullah's math class where the students were learning algebra in the context of a problem-solving exercise that not only included using their math skills but also working in teams as well as employing writing and presentation skills. Each team consisted of four or five students, with one student having the title of CEO, another chief marketing officer, and on down. The challenge they were given was to lead a company that was in competition with Apple, and they needed to make and market a product competitive with the iPhone. They used their math skills to construct a budget and business plan. As we walked from team to team, you could see the excitement and seriousness of purpose among them. As we walked into the hallway, Daniels turned to me and said, "I've never seen a math class like that!" Others have had the same impression from visiting P-TECH classrooms as critical skills are combined with a solid academic foundation to produce excellence. Some call these skills "soft skills," but I prefer to call them "essential," and it is vital that they become part of how a strong academic program is implemented.

At meetings with key influencers in politics, government, and education, I repeatedly talked about the model and its promise. One such conversation took place at a White House meeting with Gene Sperling, a top-level staffer to President Obama. Gene had been Mario Cuomo's assistant, and I knew him well from my New York City school system days. Like so many others, he felt the model had great promise and asked dozens of penetrating questions, wanting to know as much as possible about early quantifiable results. It was roll-up time to the president's 2013 State of the Union address; it was clear that this was not a passing conversation, but I knew not to depend on anything. However, the requests for information intensified, and very shortly it was clear that inclusion in the State of the Union, while not assured, was a real possibility. It was not until the day of the president's address that I received confirmation that it was definitely in the cards. While sworn to secrecy, I had enough time to call our new IBM CEO, Ginni Rometty, and a few dozen others, including Rashid Davis. The reaction from students, faculty, and so many others was enthusiastic, and from IBM, it was ecstatic.

A few weeks later, New York governor Andrew Cuomo's chief assistant with responsibility for education across the state, Jim Malatras, called to discuss a broad plan for statewide P-TECH replication and a potential announcement of the plan in the governor's State of the State address. The pledge was to have the state initiate funding for planning grants to cover the selection of 10 new P-TECH schools in each of the 10 economic development regions in the state. This would truly bring the initiative to scale, and, unlike operating district by district, put in place a strategy and program that would ensure scalability. State-level buy-in included the State Education Department, opening up P-TECH opportunities across 700 school districts, and the State University of New York (SUNY) system of over 30 community colleges, as well as the support of multiple state businesses via the Business Council of New York.

We worked through the language for the announcement and the language and quotes in the media release. Once announced, it engendered a good deal of interest and excitement. The next step, which we began immediately, was to develop a statewide steering committee to manage the governance of this initiative. The steering committee consisted of the state commissioner of education, John King, SUNY chancellor Nancy Zimpher, the governor's aide for education, Ian Rosenblum, the head of the New York State Business Council, Heather Briccetti, and myself representing IBM and their businesses. The effort, which represented the interests of business, K–12 schools, and higher education, needed its own staff, and with the support of a broad range of private funders, Robin Willner, a former IBM staffer with deep knowledge of education, was retained to coordinate the P-TECH effort across New York State. Since the launch, the support for P-TECH in New York State has been consistent and broad. Under Governor Cuomo's leadership there have been four RFPs to select and launch P-TECH schools across the state, with strong results. The chancellor of SUNY, the commissioner of education, and the business community through the State Business Council have responded to the governor's leadership and have provided the needed strong support.

After a meeting with key school districts and business leaders in Albany, the state issued a request for proposals. The responses were so on the mark that instead of 10 schools being selected as originally planned, the top 16 proposals were awarded planning grants. In September 2014, all of them opened to great fanfare with a range of industry collaborators involved. IBM was and is involved as the lead industry collaborator for Excelsior Academy, in Newburgh, New York, a community that had fallen on hard times, with crime and drug rates off the charts.

A few months later I was informed by Gene Sperling about a potential visit to P-TECH in Brooklyn by President Barack Obama. This would truly be monumental since rarely, if ever, have American presidents visited schools in New York City, though when they do, it truly is legendary. When I was growing up on the Lower East Side in New York City, I attended PS 61 on East 12th Street and Avenue B, an area known as Alphabet City, then a very depressed neighborhood. Our other local school was PS 19 on First Avenue and East 11th Street, a short walk away, and known, all these years later, as the school that President Abraham Lincoln visited. Having President Obama visit would be truly a game changer for this school—and for the model.

When President Obama was due to arrive, the streets in Crown Heights were crowded with local residents. They could not believe that the president of the United States was actually coming to Brooklyn, and not just any neighborhood, but Crown Heights. While we were getting things set up, a variety of media interviews were arranged for students and myself out in front of the school. As we exited the front door, six students and I started to engage with a TV crew when the adults on both sides of the street started chanting, "P-TECH, P-TECH, P-TECH!" Radcliffe Saddler, a P-TECH student who now works at IBM and is completing his bachelor's degree at Baruch College, was accorded the honor of introducing the president, which he did with great flair.

Of course, the logistics and everything connected to the visit were a series of very painful negotiations, but it was well worth it. President Obama visited the same math class that excited the president of Johns Hopkins. As he walked in he overheard one of the students, Kiambu Gall, who would complete his high school and AAS degrees two years ahead of schedule and accept a job at IBM, doing a President Obama impression for his fellow students. The president congratulated him on his impersonation skills. Afterward, the president walked into the combined gym and auditorium to address the crowd. As President Obama, looking incredibly happy, addressed the crowd of students, teachers, and New York politicos, along with IBM's CEO, Ginni Rometty, he made it clear that this was not about one school. He said that P-TECH ought to be an opportunity made available to every American student, and he called out IBM and its commitment and Governor Cuomo specifically for his efforts to expand the initiative across New York State.

Soon afterward, we began negotiations with a number of other states, modeling our initiatives after New York. Very rapidly, the governors of Connecticut (it launched in 2014), Colorado (2016), Maryland (2016), and Rhode Island (2016) came on board, in each instance with support from both K–12 and higher education leadership in those states, and strong support from the White House and U.S. Department of Education. In Maryland, strong support came from then Secretary of Labor Tom Perez, who became a huge advocate for P-TECH after visiting the Chicago school with Mayor Emanuel and ultimately the strong leadership of Republican governor Larry Hogan. In Rhode Island, Governor Gina Raimondo launched the program and invited business and education leaders to the launch at the state capitol. In Connecticut the governor invited business leaders to his home, and announced support for it there and at press events. And it did not stop with the United States. Importantly. the prime minister of Australia, Tony Abbott, while on a visit to the United States to meet with President Obama, also expressed interest in visiting P-TECH and collaborating with IBM to launch the program in Australia. Two schools opened in January 2015, followed by five more in 2016, and yet five more in 2017. While the prime minister would very soon thereafter give up his perch, Australian education minister Simon Birmingham took the lead in fostering P-TECH's swift adoption across the country with the full support of the next prime minister, Malcolm Turnbull. An independent not-for-profit organization, Skilling Australia, led by Nicholas Wyman, was instrumental in assisting in the embrace and operation of P-TECH in Australia.

In the next two years, the P-TECH model spread even further. Texas, with virtually unanimous support from Republican and Democratic legislators, passed a P-TECH bill providing $5 million in planning grants, making it the seventh U.S. state to embrace the P-TECH model, with schools set to open in 2019. Louisiana's governor, John Bel Edwards, has committed to Louisiana becoming the eighth state, starting with schools in Baton Rouge and East Baton Rouge with industry engagement from both IBM and Dow Chemical. Schools in Morocco opened in September 2017, after the minister of education visited a P-TECH site. Serious discussions are under way in South Africa, the United Kingdom, Italy, Canada, and South Korea, along with other U.S. states like California, New Jersey, Virginia, Washington, and North Carolina.

None of these negotiations have been easy, and none of the agreements and rollouts of schools in key states have been easy either, but the clear evidence of success in Brooklyn, followed by the other schools, was critical in getting us through those negotiations successfully.

Because education in the United States is a state function, and most of the funding and regulations are instituted at the state level, buy-in from governors, state education departments, and statewide public community college systems is critical. But because industry involvement is key, the buy-in from industry is also front and center. Today, more than 400 companies have signed on as P-TECH partners either by engaging as the sole collaborator in a school, which IBM, GlobalFoundries, and SAP have done, or as part of a consortium.

As P-TECH Brooklyn continues, it is clear that it is something special. Students benefit from an engaging academic environment and enriching workplace experiences, are on a clear road toward high school and college completion, and are ready for the demands of the workplace. As students get the opportunity to take and pass college courses, they do so at an increasing rate. Skills required in the workplace are embedded in how classes are taught. Teaching faculty make sure that problem solving, presentation, and writing are core elements in how classes are taught. A freestanding workplace learning course provided to all students reinforces that. In addition, regular structured workplace visits engage students, and mentors reinforce the fact that students are supported and have industry role models. The school also promotes a culture of achievement, which is evident to every visitor to the school. When students achieve college readiness their photographs are placed on the walls in the school hallway, and with nearly 600 students in the school the hallways have little vacant space since the photographs fill the walls.

In the summer of 2013, after P-TECH's third year, students with college credit had the opportunity to begin internships at IBM. The regular high-level visitors to the school made everyone—teachers, students, and parents—believe that something special was happening in this neighborhood. A culture of high performance, created and led by the principal, was evident. I recall a conversation I had with one of the New York City Police Department security guards who told me that Principal Davis knew every student in his school, a starkly different situation than was the case with principals in other schools she had worked in.

One would think replication of a successful school model would be relatively easy. Why not get behind what works? Well, it simply does not work that way in public education. Various model schools proliferate across states and districts, and yet embracing what works and replicating it across geographies is hard. So hard, in fact, that it rarely happens. Sometimes it doesn't happen for good reason. The program is too expensive, only works for some children rather than all, and has intractable barriers and stakeholders who are opposed to it. But in addition to the normal or expected barriers, there is one more—the notion that there is nothing applicable to my school or my district that I can learn from another.

Present an effective school in one part of town and educators will say, "Of course it works on 15th Street, but we are on 25th Street." Or, "Of course it works in a K–12 school, but we are K–12." This sums up the typical resistance to embracing change: "It has nothing to do with me." Countering such attitudes requires both a top-down and bottom-up change strategy, a serious communications and marketing plan, and a conscious effort to bring around those who might be opposed by using key influencers, relatable stories, and irrefutable data.

P-TECH has helped change the dialogue from "that school has nothing to do with me" to "that school has everything to do with me." It was the success of the initial school in Brooklyn that provided the evidence that the model works, and helped the model expand from one school to seventy and from one state to eight by the end of 2017. Brooklyn's P-TECH student and faculty attendance rates set records. The school grew, adding a cohort of about a hundred students a year. But it has been academic performance that opened people's eyes about what was possible. In a school with the highest percentage of African American male students, largely low-income, across the entire city, college completion rates were 500 percent higher than the national community college graduation rate. Significant numbers of P-TECH students complete their high school and AAS degrees one and two years ahead of schedule, with pass rates on college courses at over 90 percent. Importantly, the high school dropout rate was near zero as well. Students either take their AAS degree and enroll in public or private four-year programs to continue their path to a bachelor's degree, or accept jobs at IBM. Many have a job at IBM and continue their education at the same time.

Increasingly, P-TECH success is maintained across geographies. As other P-TECH schools complete one, two, three, four years of operations, their successes show that Brooklyn's successes are not an anomaly. In Newburgh, New York, under the leadership of principal Kevin Rothman, by the end of the program's third year, roughly 25 percent of students are on track to complete their AAS in cybersecurity in four, not six years. Similar results are evident in the P-TECH school in Norwalk, Connecticut, where under Karen Amaker's leadership 20 percent of the entry-level class will graduate with both degrees in four years and 50 percent of the total student body of over 300 hundred students are on the honor roll.

Key influencers who have visited Brooklyn P-TECH, inspired by what they saw, also have played a vital role in replication. Visits by national and international educators are a regular occurrence, as they are at the schools in Chicago, Newburgh, and Norwalk. Shortly after Secretary of Labor Perez visited the P-TECH school in Chicago, he spoke at a National Governors Association conference and urged all governors to replicate the model. After his visit to the school in Brooklyn, Secretary of Education Arne Duncan urged governors in Connecticut and Colorado to adopt the model. I had the pleasure of taking New York's lieutenant governor, Kathy Hochul, to visit the Newburgh school. During a classroom observation, she asked a ninth grader to tell her what she had learned that week that she thought was particularly valuable. Without missing a beat, the student responded by saying she had learned how to do an "elevator pitch" from her IBM mentor, which she then recited. Influencers like these, while not making decisions about education on the ground, provide clarity and weight to the education discourse, and with their strong vocal support, have helped propel the model forward.

Changing Federal Policy

Rapid expansion across the United States and in several countries requires more than state-by-state and country-by-country expansion. While creating 70 or even 100 schools would be noteworthy, true reform requires an infusion of steroids to significantly and dramatically accelerate the rate and nature of its expansion. In this effort we targeted an alteration in the federal funding source for career and technical education, and the creation of a federal model along with funding, to spread the P-TECH model much, much further.

While not as significant as the engine behind the creation of Social Security, the changes sought on the federal level for all career and technical education modeled after P-TECH were very important. Vocational education in America has traditionally been thought of as a second-class opportunity for students who do not have the ability to complete an academic high school program, let alone attend or complete college, whether a two- or four-year program. Students who attended vocational programs had the opportunity to learn skills to perform a specific job, but that basically was it. Support for vocational education came from local school districts and states, but the federal Carl D. Perkins Vocational and Technical Education Act, first authorized in 1984, distributed funding across the states to provide the added resources for materials, supplies, and instruction. The last reauthorization of the act was over a decade ago, in 2006, with federal funding largely distributed across the states on a per capita basis, meaning that a state received funding based on its total pupil count, regardless of what specifically was done with the funding. Largely what was done was what had been done the year, or decades, before.

To replicate P-TECH across the United States beyond 100 or even 200 schools, which is the goal over the next three to four years, we determined we needed to energize a broad constituency to support a change in the federal law and the way in which funds are distributed. Most businesses lobby for federal, state, or local changes that directly benefit them in the short term. The change here would be something that would benefit business to be sure, by addressing the need for higher skill levels among America's youth, but the benefit would be long-term, and those interested in supporting such changes would expand beyond business to include education groups, labor, civil rights organizations, and student groups. The core agenda addressed the fundamental elements of P-TECH but was done in a way that created a big and broad tent to accommodate different interests, both programmatic and geographic.

The agenda we settled upon would focus on preparation for careers linked directly to labor market data to ensure that preparation would be linked to high-demand and high-wage career opportunities, like information technology, health care, finance, and advanced manufacturing.

Second, there would need to be a focus on the link between high school and college. Ending school with only a high school diploma would continue to wall off that opportunity—an economic imperative in this twenty-first-century economy. Third, there would need to be a focus on experiential learning, like paid internships and workplace learning opportunities, to fully reinforce the importance of workplace skills. Fourth, there would need to be metrics for performance, encouraging districts and states to capture and publish outcomes.

This wide tent included the major national business associations like the Business Roundtable and the U.S. Chamber of Commerce, as well as state and local business groups. Other supporters included organized labor such as the American Federation of Teachers (AFT), civil rights groups such as the NAACP and 100 Black Men, and local districts, colleges, and trade associations. Building broad support required endless calls and meetings but ultimately succeeded with over 400 signatories to a letter outlining support for the Perkins reform. The next step was to approach legislators at the federal level in both the House and Senate, and on both sides of the aisle, to outline the changes sought. On one day of visits to Senate members, I walked into the offices of Senator Bob Casey of Pennsylvania, along with AFT president Randi Weingarten, to make the case for the core elements of change in the federal law. The senator said this was the first time representatives from business and labor were in his office at the same time and both of them on the same page.

Moving this idea forward was no simple task and involved multiple meetings, a media strategy, and persistence over several years. Before the 2016 summer recess, the Perkins reauthorization bill passed the U.S. House of Representatives by an astounding vote of 405 to 5. It died in the Senate in the fall of 2016 due to the divisions resulting from the presidential election, but passed the House again by a wide bipartisan margin in the spring of 2017. And in the fall of 2017, a letter urging passage in the Senate was signed by 60 of the 100 U.S. senators, demonstrating broad support. I'm confident that action in the Senate and a signature by the president will happen, though it will take time and consistent advocacy.

Of course, this is only the beginning. There are other federal programs that should be changed, including the Federal Work-Study program, and the U.S. Apprenticeship program under the Department of Labor. Work-study is very dear to my heart. Federal Work-Study was initiated by President Johnson as part of his War on Poverty in the late 1960s, providing work opportunities where 80 percent of a student's wages were paid by federal funds. Higher education institutions paid the remaining 20 percent, with students largely working on campus in libraries and cafeterias. When I worked at City Hall under Mayor Lindsay in New York, I ran the Urban Corps, a national version of the Peace Corps, in which over 10,000 students from over 100 colleges and universities across the country had full-time summer and part-time school-year internships with city agencies. In some instances, they helped manage whole agencies. A group of interns, college students, and law students staffed the borough offices of the Department of Consumer Affairs and were hugely productive. Our effort to give students real-world work experience in the public sector was an innovation at the time. While beginning in New York City and championed by Mayor Lindsay, it eventually spread to over 100 cities across the country. But by the 1980s, work-study funding cuts during the Reagan administration meant that off-campus work limited cheap on-campus labor, and as a result off-campus work under the law was virtually eliminated.

P-TECH's success offers an opportunity to revisit work-study, and use it to stimulate high-quality, high-wage work opportunities for students off campus. The federal subsidy could support 50 percent of eligible students' wages, with employers picking up the rest and offering real opportunities for internships and practical experience. Hundreds of thousands of students could benefit, making paid internships and experiential learning the norm, not the exception. Similarly, apprenticeship programs also could be brought into the twenty-first century, focusing on expanded opportunities in higher-wage jobs, and judging providers based on outcomes rather than process. Countries like Norway and Switzerland have demonstrated the advantage of the apprenticeship model, and this is the right time to expand it in the United States and make it more effective. Reauthorization of the Perkins Act, work-study, and apprenticeship programs offer opportunities to reshape how billions of federal funding dollars are used, producing higher value, better skills, and greater opportunity for many more Americans.

Walking and Chewing Gum at the Same Time

By September 2017, just six years since its launch, P-TECH could in many ways be considered well established. It represents a shift in American education around the pathway from high school to college to career. Its design to radically address low rates of college readiness and college completion in a way that focuses on the skills crisis and income inequality required a multifaceted strategy. Initiating new programs in additional states was critical to demonstrating momentum and scalability. Attracting new states to embrace P-TECH to demonstrate broad and bipartisan interest was key as well. While initiating the program in international geographies may have seemed to some as a distraction, it actually reinforced the broad applicability of the model. Perhaps most important, we needed to devote significant attention to make certain that existing schools and legacy populations of students maintained the promise of higher rates of achievement, college readiness, college completion, and skilled employment. Since there is no established governmental effort to replicate the schools across the United States, the continued state-by-state push fell to IBM.

One would perhaps expect that if a model was built on data and examples of what works and delivered strong results, continuing support, with tweaks, of course, to build on strengths and correct any weaknesses would be relatively easy. That is certainly the model of American entrepreneurs across multiple industries. However, it is not common practice in education. Yet following similar assumptions in bringing about change in education is a mistake, and those who follow that assumption are doomed to fail.

Certain overarching political issues changed the landscape as well. In the initial Brooklyn P-TECH school, the support provided by Mayor Bloomberg, along with school chancellors Klein and then Dennis Walcott, was changed significantly with the mayoral election in 2015. While Bill de Blasio's first mayoral campaign included a pledge to start another dozen P-TECH schools were he elected, and he attended President Obama's school visit in 2013 in his role as the city public advocate, and the support for P-TECH expansion in the city continues, the New York City Department of Education has focused away from closing failed schools and reopening new ones, which was one link to expanding P-TECH. Efforts in education in the city also shifted focus a bit away from high school reform, instead to a focus on expanding and making pre-K programs universal. High school reform and the P-TECH strategy for achieving it, while still supported, moved a bit lower on the totem pole. However, based on the success, it is clear that there is strong support for adding P-TECH schools in the future.

In addition to the overarching political changes, while the incredible attention focused on P-TECH contributed enormously to its success, it also engendered another reaction: jealousy and antagonism from those who like to throw stones at successes they feel are not theirs. This was a negative by-product of presidential attention, a cover story in *Time* magazine, a PBS documentary, and more. In year four of the program, CUNY and its partner community colleges began to alter the rules governing P-TECH. When the school opened, students who took college courses were treated as nonmatriculated students, so if they failed a course, it was not counted toward their grade point average. To graduate from any CUNY program, students had to have a 2.0 grade point average (or letter grade C), and over the initial four years of the school, only 3 percent of students ever received a failing grade. At the four-year mark, we celebrated our first six graduates (who graduated with their high school and AAS degrees in four years rather than six), with three going on to earn their bachelor's degree and three hired by IBM. Other students had earned significant college credit, and were performing strongly.

With no consultation with its partners, CUNY changed its policy, deciding to treat P-TECH students as matriculated students. Our principal, Rashid Davis, was rightfully disturbed that he was not consulted in advance, and we fought on his behalf to change it. While the policy change required work to explain to students and their families and reinforce changes at the school level, it was implemented and actually had few, if any, consequences on students' ability to earn their high school diploma and associate's degree on time or at an accelerated pace.

CUNY later attempted to alter the rules to determine when a student could take a credit-bearing course. When the school first opened, students were eligible to take a college course if they passed one college readiness benchmark. If the student was college-ready in math, they could take a math course with college credit; the same was true in English. In year six, CUNY changed its policy, again with no consultation, to require students to pass both the math and English benchmarks before they could access *any* college course despite the data that demonstrated that students who passed only one benchmark succeeded in college courses, and the vast majority ultimately passed the second benchmark. Rashid was again disturbed by this change as well, but in this case after discussions we were able to get CUNY and City Tech to reconsider the change. We requested that if a student passed one benchmark and had the principal's support based on review of other criteria connected to academics and behavior, Rashid could recommend a waiver and allow the student to take college courses. Looking back at the data, it was clear that of those students who met one of the two benchmarks, their college grades were high. These are but two examples, but it demonstrates that even in the initial and extremely successful school, it was important to monitor activities to put the interests of the students first.

Operational challenges were not restricted to P-TECH in Brooklyn. At Norwalk Early College Academy (NECA), the first grades 9–12 school in Connecticut, issues also arose. A critical part of P-TECH is the culture of high achievement, with a belief that all students will get to their degrees regardless of where they start. That culture must permeate the school, students, faculty, and administration alike. Creating that culture within NECA, which is a school within a larger high school, was challenging at first. Karen Amaker, the house principal of NECA, reported to the larger school principal and found messaging the differences between NECA and the larger Norwalk High School challenging. She did not have authority over her budget, nor did she have a dedicated guidance counselor. All these issues were worked out after meetings with key stakeholders, including Norwalk Public Schools superintendent Steven Adamowski, who embraced the program and lent the school and Principal Amaker his strong support, as did the president of Norwalk Community College, David Levinson. One aspect was not resolved (as of this writing) that was the most important issue: the original commitment made by Governor Dannel Malloy to ensure that the grades 9–12 model would be free to students and their families. Rather than see the model collapse, the president of Norwalk Community College, NECA's community college partner, stepped up to the plate and assumed full responsibility for the tuition bill. NECA leadership has insured that none of these challenges derailed the school's incredible success, where roughly a quarter of the initial cohort of students are on track to complete their high school and two-year college degrees two full years ahead of schedule, and a full 50 percent of students are on the honor roll.

In Chicago, after signing a memorandum of understanding with Chicago Public Schools and City Colleges of Chicago outlining core commitments to the P-TECH model, a year later, our partners wanted to renegotiate. The district would commit to free tuition to only those students who after year four had a GPA of 2.5 or higher, which meant that the most vulnerable students would not receive the ongoing supports needed to earn their degree. After IBM broached the notion that it might have to leave the partnership rather than stay in one that was not honoring the original commitment (a far from easy decision given our commitment to the students and teachers at the Sarah E. Goode STEM Academy), Mayor Emanuel intervened and committed to free tuition for all students. However, students in Chicago must graduate at year four from high school, and then have the option to attend any community college in the city, making it more challenging to follow and support students. Nevertheless, the success of the school continues with the mayor's strong support and the evidence of high graduation rates, growing college completion rates, high attendance and college readiness, and pass rates on college courses. Of course, another major element in success at Goode was the replacement of the initial principal with Armando Rodriguez, whose strong leadership has been critical in achieving success by students. Nevertheless, these examples across districts and states demonstrate a fact about school reform: you cannot take your eye off the ball.

Despite what has taken place behind the scenes, the performance of P-TECH schools has been more than positive. These are open enrollment schools serving largely low-income populations, and have college completion rates that blow past national averages, as does the college readiness of students. Pass rates on college courses taken while students are on the high school registers are in excess of 90 percent; attendance is also higher than district averages; and dropout rates are extremely low and in some cases virtually nonexistent. Perhaps most important, no student in any of the schools has taken a remedial non-credit-bearing course once they attend a four-year college or university. It would be difficult to come to any other conclusion than that the program is successful and working in struggling communities across the United States. However, the story is best told in the words of those it is designed to serve: the students themselves.

Student Stories

When P-TECH opened its doors in the fall of 2011, students like Leslieanne John and Radcliffe Saddler hardly expected that they would complete a two-year college degree, enter a four-year institution with a strong academic record, get a job at IBM, and do all that in less than the six years expected. Leslieanne completed her combined high school and college degree in four and a half years. She now works at IBM as an internship coordinator for the company while attending Brooklyn College part-time to get her bachelor's degree. She often speaks to students about her P-TECH experience. She also had an opportunity to accompany IBM chairman and CEO Ginni Rometty on a visit to the White House, along with P-TECH graduate Janiel Richards, to stand

and explain, in front of President Trump and German chancellor Angela Merkel, the unique benefits of P-TECH. Radcliffe Saddler had the honor of introducing President Obama when he visited P-TECH and now works at IBM in digital design while completing his bachelor's degree at Baruch College. He too completed his high school and associate's degrees in four years. ShuDon Brown also completed her degrees in four years and has a scholarship to William Peace College in North Carolina, where she also interned at IBM. Oscar Tendilla completed his dual degrees in three and a half years and is now attending Cornell University on a full scholarship. His mother received her GED, urged on by Oscar, during the same month that he was awarded his AAS in computer science. BryAnn Sandy completed her degree in three and a half years, is a track and field champion in the girls' 400 meters, and is now attending Georgetown University, also on a full scholarship. Joel Duran is at SUNY Albany, completing his bachelor's degree ahead of schedule as well. He has had internships at IBM, and at SUNY Albany has served as a mentor for other P-TECH graduates who followed him to SUNY Albany. Chigozie Okorie graduated in four years and works full-time at IBM. David Caliste, another early graduate, works for IBM in Atlanta after completing his program two years early. The stories are adding up. All are students of color from low-income communities. Based on their profiles at the end of grade eight, at least on paper, their prospects did not look all that encouraging, and yet their accomplishments speak for themselves. The fact that each student had a mentor at IBM, a paid internship at the company, and opportunities to progress in college courses while still on the high school register and not just take a few college courses but achieve an associate's degree concurrent with their high school diploma demonstrates that assumptions based on race or income levels can be thwarted with the appropriate opportunity and consistent support.

Let me focus a bit on one of the students in the first class at P-TECH. Gabriel Rosa's parents are immigrants who arrived in the United States from the Dominican Republic. They immigrated in the 1970s and '80s, and after a short stay in the Washington Heights section of Manhattan, then the largest Dominican community in New York City, they moved to Bedford-Stuyvesant in Brooklyn, which at the time was a very distressed community. This is the same community where IBM opened a plant in the late 1960s. Gabriel began school in Bedford-Stuyvesant at PS 256, but his mother was dissatisfied with the quality of the program, and shortly thereafter got him moved to a higher-level elementary school in Brooklyn Heights, PS 8, where he started in third grade. Gabriel's father took him to school every day on the subway, and he was picked up by his mom. For sixth grade, he was moved, again at his mother's behest, to MS 113 in Fort Greene, Brooklyn, where he initially struggled both academically and socially. By eighth grade, he had focused very little of his time on high school choices and options (in New York City, students identify their top 12 choices and an algorithm makes the assignment). Gabriel filled out an application listing eight choices, some screened programs, others unscreened, but he got into none of them.

Gabriel's father had heard about P-TECH and encouraged the guidance counselor at Gabriel's middle school to see if there was a way for him to attend. While he had gotten no formal acceptance, on the first day of school, Gabriel simply walked the mile and a half from his home to P-TECH on Albany Avenue. He was a bit put off by the metal detectors and New York City Police Department staff in the lobby of the school but was thrilled that there was an admissions packet waiting for him at the school. While the first few weeks at school were a challenge, Gabriel pretty quickly settled in and realized he would be able to move at his own pace, eventually taking and passing college courses with rapidity. By the end of ninth grade, Gabriel began to hit his stride and realized that he could not only do well at P-TECH, but could accelerate. His parents continued to encourage him, and his academic performance got better and better. He had an IBM mentor and made a big success of his summer internship at IBM, where under the guidance of Maria Arbusto, a director at IBM, he succeeded beyond all expectations. As he entered twelfth grade, it was clear that he would graduate with both his high school diploma and his AAS that spring with flying colors. After media interviews and a high-profile college graduation ceremony at Brooklyn's Barclays Center, Gabriel settled down at an IBM job in digital design and took courses at Hunter College toward a bachelor's degree after work and on weekends. He was promoted after two years with IBM. He mentors other P-TECH students and is skilled and mature beyond his age. In fact, he is taking the lead in developing a P-TECH alumni network. P-TECH for Gabriel Rosa was a life-changing, life-shaping, and transformational experience.

Results

No education innovation, or innovation of any kind for that matter, can be judged without examining outcome data. Yes, there are hundreds of students whose lives have been improved, with stories that tug at the heartstrings, but given the focus on one of the nation's most significant problems, what are the results? P-TECH schools have significantly higher attendance rates and high school graduation rates than other schools in their districts. None of the students have ever taken even one non-credit-bearing remedial college course; college readiness figures are off the charts. P-TECH students take college courses in high school with a better than 90 percent pass rate, with 60 percent of students earning As or Bs on those courses. The percentage of P-TECH students earning Ds is in the low single digits. While the Brooklyn P-TECH school is the only one at this point to have completed year six, its college completion rate is 400 percent higher than the national average for all students and 500 percent higher compared with low-income students.

Chicago has completed year five, and Newburgh and Norwalk, under the strong leadership of principals like Kevin Rothman, Karen Amaker, and Armando Rodriguez, have completed year three, and all three have results that mirror the results in Brooklyn.

Among the states implementing this model, New York State has the most comprehensive approach. With the leadership of the governor and strong support from education leadership, P-TECH schools stretch across the state, covering all 10 economic regions. Some schools have a single industry partner like IBM or SAP, while others engage with a network of companies, large, medium, and small, often focused on a geography. In 2014, the state, through a competitive RFP process, selected and launched 16 P-TECH schools, and by 2017 those schools already had results that mirrored the Brooklyn trajectory. Based on college readiness and college course completion, the projected college completion rate is on track to be over 300 percent higher than the national average. Serving a student population that is 70 percent free-lunch eligible, college pass rates while students are still on the high school registers exceed 90 percent, with more than 60 percent of the students who passed their college courses earning As or Bs, and not one single student ever having had to take a non-credit-bearing remedial course.

By projecting these results, achieved in urban, suburban, and rural schools, serving the most underserved populations, and doing so within all the rules and regulations governing public education, it is clear that if these results were achieved nationwide, we would solve the nation's college readiness and college completion challenge by a wide margin and successfully address America's skills crisis. It would allow the nearly $3 billion spent on remedial courses to be reallocated to hire more and better teachers. Tax revenue generated from higher wages earned by better-trained and better-skilled employees would produce significant economic benefits. Simply put, it would bring America a significantly brighter future.

Engaging the Company over the Long Term

As IBM enters year eight of its involvement in the P-TECH reform, it is essential to review its performance, and the program's connections to the company and to other companies as well. Obviously, we begin with the fact that the model is a success, has expanded, and is sustainable given the strong support it has from government, education leaders, labor, and industry. But as the investment grows and as the years go by, we need to quantify the ability to garner the continued support of the company, its leadership—including at the board level—its employees, and the public. So let's examine the case for company continued commitment to P-TECH.

IBM, like all technology companies, has a significant interest in the recruitment of top talent. To only recruit from top colleges and universities is a zero-sum game. Companies need to diversify their talent pools to enable innovation, and this can only be done by utilizing the most effective and efficient models of recruitment, and by expanding the number of individuals recruited. P-TECH connects directly to IBM's talent acquisition strategy, which IBM chairman and CEO Ginni Rometty characterizes as "new collar" jobs, defined as not white-collar or blue-collar and requiring more than a high school diploma but not necessarily a four-year degree. To find such talent, IBM needs a diverse pipeline and a cost-efficient model for finding the best talent. Since the largest investment in P-TECH is made by repurposing existing public-sector investments, P-TECH connects directly to IBM's business strategy. Like all companies, IBM and the entire technology industry are challenged to diversify their employee population. P-TECH recruits qualified minorities and women, drawing on a new pool of employees from different economic and social backgrounds.

In 2015, Rana Foroohar, the reporter from *Time* magazine who wrote the cover story about P-TECH and IBM, spoke at a Silicon Valley conclave and openly urged companies to do more to diversify their workforce. Just as IBM and other companies did in the 1960s with pressure from government and the public, IT companies cannot sit back without addressing the lack of women and minorities in their workforce. Rana urged Silicon Valley companies to follow IBM's lead. P-TECH provided IBM with branding and communications validation for its work, but unlike other companies that were doing precious little to address this problem and were forced to fund anywhere from a few million to tens of millions of dollars for minority scholarships, IBM, because of its P-TECH partnership, did not have to announce any such donations. And a lack of diversity is hardly unique to technology companies. It is a concern and problem across most industries.

In addition to addressing the need for talent, diverse talent specifically, P-TECH also gives IBM employees the opportunities to engage, proudly and meaningfully. IBMers have volunteered their time mentoring thousands of P-TECH students across states, localities, and countries and serving as mentors and worksite visit hosts. IBMers also manage interns, helping develop young talent while getting help on actual work projects. In particular, for many IBM employees, serving as a mentor becomes an extremely rewarding part of their work life. Robyn Gantt is a human resources executive at IBM. She is African American and grew up in Newburgh, New York, site of one of the P-TECH schools. She has served as a student mentor from day one. She is a role model for her mentee, has guided her through the initial three years of her P-TECH experience, and helped support her summer internship after eleventh grade. Gantt supports her student mentee's education experiences and in turn her mentee excels in time management, completed team projects, and in her college courses. She has earned enough college credits to be on track to receive her high school diploma and AAS degree in under five years total.

Given all the benefits—the long-term and labor-intensive commitment to P-TECH, navigating multiple domestic and international geographies, changes in hiring practices, governmental and policy hurdles, and employee engagement and support—continued support from IBM and other companies appears to be well justified given the demonstrable and measurable benefits to the company. Call it a return on investment.

Lessons Learned

P-TECH will continue its rise in 2018, with over 120 schools implementing this program across eight states and three other countries, benefiting over 25,000 students. And that is just the start. It likely will continue to expand and is on track to serve over 100,000 students across the United States and globally within three years.

There are numerous lessons learned from IBM's efforts involving P-TECH. Lesson number one is that school reform is not impossible but needs collaboration, especially with the private sector. However, real, sustainable, and lasting reform requires a deep knowledge of the system and how it works; a reform program must have as few built-in barriers to expansion as possible and a specifically articulated and designed replication plan built into the design. Since public education is run by public institutions, and funded by those institutions, a reform initiative that engages the private sector must be designed and delivered in a collaborative fashion with benchmarks and metrics to assess and evaluate progress. It must connect to broader policy issues and include key stakeholders.

For the private-sector collaborator, it needs to be achievable, marketable, and affordable, with a return on investment, however that may be defined. It should offer opportunities to engage employees in meaningful ways. It must have a positive impact on the company brand. It must build relationships at the highest levels of government—presidents and prime ministers, governors and mayors—that offer positive benefit for the business as well. Perhaps most important, initiatives should link to a core business and societal issue—the skills crisis in the case of P-TECH—that connects to the company bottom line and ultimately builds the next generation of diverse talent.

IBM Launches Teacher Advisor with Watson

The launch and subsequent success of P-TECH was not the only egg in IBM's corporate social responsibility basket. When IBM innovated the use of artificial intelligence, or Watson cognitive computing technology, to win the game show *Jeopardy!* in 2011, it was clear that this transformative technology was a potential game changer. Shortly thereafter, working with some of the most renowned medical centers across the United States, IBM built an oncology advisor using Watson to augment the knowledge of cancer doctors, enabling them to implement more effective strategies, along with targeted and effective treatment plans.

Within a year after the work began on the medical application of the technology, IBM brought together a group of over a hundred of the most prominent education leaders in the country to Roosevelt House in New York City, where in the 1930s President Roosevelt and Frances Perkins discussed the launch of Social Security in the home's library. After viewing a demonstration of the Watson technology, I led a brainstorming session about how this technology might be used to improve student outcomes. After fits and starts about whether the technology might fuel a more effective student testing system or provide special education students with customized support, rather quickly the discussion turned to how it might improve the quality of teaching. If Watson could become a coach and advisor to doctors, why couldn't it do the same for teachers? Unlike doctors or other professionals like lawyers, engineers, or accountants, teachers are often isolated from colleagues, working on their own in their classroom—and certainly do not have cutting-edge technologies at their fingertips. Their workspace is with students, behind a closed door. While research shows that teacher instruction is effectively improved through observation, feedback, and practice, rarely do they have any access to a mentor or any sort of support to improve their practice.

At the end of several hours of give-and-take, the clear consensus was that if Watson technology could become a personalized coach for teachers, it might be a game changer for educators and students. Our initial subject area would be elementary math, starting with grade three, during which students learn multiplication, division, and fractions, the foundational concepts of algebra.

Shortly after the session, I brought the idea for Teacher Advisor with Watson to IBM CEO Ginni Rometty and with her strong support began to create a plan to bring it to life. An IBM research team was assembled on the technical side. As with all IBM's philanthropic efforts, we teamed with subject matter experts, forming a partnership with a new not-for-profit education reform organization, now called UnboundEd. It is staffed with the educational professionals central to the success of EngageNY, a New York State Education Department program to support the implementation of key aspects of the New York State Board of Regents Reform Agenda, including the Common Core. Teacher Advisor was conceived as a resource that would assist teachers in obtaining high-quality lesson plans integrated with pedagogical strategies using video, annotated for easy use. With the power of Watson, the resource also would serve as a personal coaching tool, with the goal of enabling teachers to provide students of a range of learning needs with individual instruction. I sought the strong buy-in and support of the American Federation of Teachers through its leader, Randi Weingarten, and was delighted when she recognized its value and threw her support to it. While Teacher Advisor was always intended to be a free resource for teachers, I understood that teachers may not want to sign up for a solution with only IBM branding. To make it a more inclusive solution, I sought and won the support of private foundations, including the Ford Foundation, the Carnegie Foundation, and the Stavros Niarchos Foundation; as a group, we were able to engage hundreds of teachers to help train Watson to address their needs and understand the language of elementary school math.

Our long-term goal was to use Watson technology to essentially become a personal coach for teachers—indeed, the most talented and effective coach imaginable, providing the best lesson plans, teaching strategies, advice, and support. Importantly, Teacher Advisor would need to be nonjudgmental; it would not be offered by a school district or state but directly to the individual teacher, nor would it be used to evaluate teacher performance. Rather it would be built by teachers for teachers with no ulterior motive.

Simultaneous with launching this effort, we also felt it wise to put together an advisory group of supporters, consisting of education influencers, to demonstrate that unlike so many other education reforms, this was one that had minimal detractors and a maximum number of supporters and advocates. Within a year, Teacher Advisor was ready to pilot, and while it went through several iterations, with many flaws in the development, it received significant positive feedback. Teachers were able to do tasks online that were truly an asset, including the ability to customize a lesson plan to meet the needs of their particular class. The resources integrated hundreds of high-quality lessons with pedagogical videos from multiple sources (all open source).

In the fall of 2017, after a pilot involving over 1,000 teachers and with strong support from school districts and states, and endorsement from two U.S. secretaries of education, Arne Duncan and John King, and numerous education school deans, Teacher Advisor was launched for all teachers. Within a week, 2,500 new teachers had registered, and it received over 25 million impressions on social media. Within the next month the number of teachers registered on the site increased to 7,500. Support for this initiative is broad-based. The National School Boards Association, the Education Commission of the States, the National Board for Professional Teaching Standards, Achieve, and so many others have helped engage teachers and school leaders. Early results are encouraging, with teachers excited and spreading the word. But as with P-TECH or any education reform, total success cannot be evident on day one or week one. It will need long-term and sustained support and continued improvement.

Teacher Advisor's success is best explained in the words of Christine Manna. Christine is a New Jersey teacher who also serves as a math coach. She has worked with teachers across grade levels in her district, and she told me that she feels that many elementary school teachers she interacts with regularly are in the classroom under pressure. Many have not been trained specifically in math, and thus she feels it is particularly important that they receive additional support to help them understand math curricula and standards more explicitly and to strengthen their instructional practices to more effectively meet the needs of their students.

We had asked Christine, along with dozens and dozens of teachers across the United States, to assist in the development of Teacher Advisor from its earliest incarnation. She said, "When I first heard about the tool, I really wasn't sure what to expect. While the earliest version of Teacher Advisor showed tremendous potential, and the idea that the power of

Watson-augmented intelligence could be focused on supporting educators directly was innovative, the first prototype was a little clunky. It worked, but it needed to be easier to use and more visually appealing. I wasn't shy about voicing my criticisms and I was prepared not to be heard. But as soon as I saw the revised version months later my eyes blew up! The IBM team has really listened to me, along with a diverse group of fellow teachers, working with us every step of the way to incorporate all of our suggestions into the tool. What gets me really excited on top of the fact that it is so desperately needed is IBM demonstrating a commitment to giving us something teachers need and want, and it's free and totally confidential. The content meets diverse student needs; there are activities with heavy visualization that can help English Language Learners, along with activities incorporating more complex language for more advanced students, and the resources are vetted, not just a wiki. You get the best of breed resources whether you are a beginning teacher or a veteran or someone teaching a grade for the first time, and because it's cognitive, it will get smarter. I think it's one of the most exciting developments in teaching that I've seen in my eleven years as a teacher."

Eric Wisznewski is another enthusiastic fan of Teacher Advisor. Eric teaches in Newburgh, New York, and has been a teacher for 11 years. His views are very similar to those of Christine. According to Eric, teachers are under enormous pressure to deliver results and often don't get the type of assistance and support they need. Specifically, he highlighted the frustration of delivering a lesson in the classroom, and at the end of the day realizing that it simply did not work, either in total or for certain students, with teachers essentially being on their own to figure out what to do next. Eric values the fact that the content, whether lessons or teaching strategies, is vetted and integrated in a user-friendly way. Finally, the fact that Teacher Advisor learns and improves the more teachers use it makes it even more special.

This is one of the most transformational aspects of this effort to improve teaching quality and thus student achievement—the fact that because it uses artificial intelligence, it learns and improves with use. Unlike a standard product, its ability and its assets consistently improve. When you buy a car, you decide what features you want before purchase, and whatever you buy, you are stuck with. Artificial intelligence means that new features and enhanced performance will in fact be a core element of the solution.

Will it be a game changer—something on the level of what is being provided to cancer doctors not only in the United States but around the world? It certainly holds that promise. What's critical is that the "build it and they will come" philosophy is not true. Even this meaningful technology requires significant support from key stakeholders—all those who are needed to support it, along with all those who would have opposed it—to share. And while artificial intelligence continues to learn and improve as it is used, the technology also requires ongoing advancement so that it evolves and matures.

The Skills Crisis Goes Far Beyond the Entry Level

Addressing the critical issue of employment skills in the twenty-first century goes far beyond the issue of entry-level job opportunities to the need for higher levels of education and skills. Here again government has a clear responsibility, but the governmental approach via the apprenticeship program funded by the U.S. Department of Labor is, by any measure of analysis, largely ineffective. With roughly $200 million in competitive grants, the program has no clear focus, restricts funding to a small range of options, and is not matched with the largest set of needs based on labor market data or geography. Once more the gap in creating effective solutions marrying the needs of business and society has been left unaddressed.

One intriguing and promising model, called Workforce 2020, was developed in 2017 by AT&T. Interestingly, just two years earlier, the company suffered a disruptive strike by its employees, largely over wages and the cost of health benefits in a rapidly changing and highly competitive industry. The strike was settled amicably, but shortly thereafter the company turned its focus to an even larger labor problem coupled with an innovative solution. Internal company analysis showed that of a workforce of 250,000 people, roughly 40 percent of current jobs would likely disappear over the next decade. These job losses will not be the result of global competition, but the result of a shift in the company business model from hardware to software, putting a premium on a different kind of technical and professional skills. Were the company to plan for this shift in the workforce in traditional ways, it might force early retirements coupled with what companies call "resource actions," a benign phrase that means firing workers. This strategy has a huge cost, including to the company's reputation, especially for a company with a union workforce. Concurrent with a strategy to shed its workforce, the company would have to embark on an expensive multiyear effort to recruit people with the right skills and education to fill new job demands.

Workforce 2020 represented a stark contrast from prior responses to changes in the skill level required by large numbers of jobs in the company. It resulted instead in a major investment in retraining by the company. Portions of the retraining developed in a customized fashion by the company take place during the workday and are incorporated into an employee's work schedule, allowing them the opportunity to expand their skills, but a large portion of added education and training also takes place voluntarily on an employee's own time. This way, while the company makes a significant contribution to enhancing skills and preserving jobs, employees do the same. The effort is not "one size fits all"; it focuses on the diverse individual skills and needs, incorporating education and skills tied to individual positions and job categories. The delivery of the model is diverse as well, providing training through online courses, stretch assignments, internships, and/or tuition reimbursement.

If AT&T is able to demonstrate that it can improve skills and retrain its existing workforce in a way that results in savings above the investment needed, it can be a model for other companies and industries to follow.

Citizen Diplomacy

While education and a skilled labor force are top priorities for many corporations, they are not the only ones. In an increasingly global economy, there is another issue of critical importance that companies can and must play, what I would characterize as "citizen diplomacy." Global companies need to demonstrate their ability to address the broader role of corporations across a range of societal issues, and this is especially crucial in promoting stability in the developing world. This critical societal issue is directly connected to a company's global business interests with respect to the talent pipeline, combined with the interests of their employees, the communities they serve and/or hope to serve, shareholders, political leaders, and the media.

In 2006, IBM's then chairman and CEO Sam Palmisano authored an article in *Foreign Affairs* magazine opining that the business model at IBM was changing, and such change would spread across industries. IBM began a journey to reinvent the company alongside a significantly different business model to become a globally integrated company. What did this mean? Well, most companies that operated globally had a series of siloed organizational structures in individual countries. IBM Australia and IBM Brazil, for example, each had structures where employees and executives served clients in those countries. Operating across well over 100 countries, geographic units had their own operating structure, including budget, human resources, operations, information technology, communications, marketing, and more. In a "flat" world, this model was out of date and in need of reform. A globally integrated company meant that people in one geography needed to collaborate and partner with others in another geography, and also needed to understand the interests of clients both in their locations as well as in others. This required a knowledge base about the global economy and especially geographies in the developing world. In the history of citizen engagement and community involvement, historically companies only established programs and a presence in those geographies where they had an existing employee base and client interests. The idea of expanding and using corporate responsibility as a way of opening or "making" a market was not on their radar screens.

The IBM approach was to think through a new model, where potential leaders within the company would be offered an opportunity to acquire the adaptability skills, problem-solving capabilities, and advanced understanding of complex emerging markets. They would do this firsthand, while providing government and civil society interests in key growth market geographies with tangible and significant assistance as they attempted to grow their economies.

IBM began by examining a set of existing models within the company, within other companies, and in the public and not-for-profit sectors as a basis for developing a model that could effectively address these core elements, and do so in a scalable and sustainable fashion.

The most prominent existing model was the concept of the international assignment. When companies, IBM included, attempted to address the need for cultural adaptability and skills involving international markets, they very often assigned an experienced senior leader within the company's executive ranks and offered them an international assignment for a year or more. The position the individual took often would involve handling a critical management function, from country general manager to head of budget, human resources, legal, or sales. Because individuals offered such assignments were fairly high-paid executives (many senior executives, many nearing retirement), who required travel and moving and living expenses for them and their families, the cost of such assignments was high, especially when a company factored in moving and living expenses, tax consequences, and the cost of replacements. In a study done for the Conference Board, on average each international assignment reached in excess of $1 million per participant per year. The goal of such assignments was to bring conformity to a location and focus almost solely on the needs of the company and bottom-line results.

In contrast, IBM needed a scalable model that would be low-cost, would focus on emerging leaders, and would provide a triple benefit: assist the company, assist local geographies, and meet the needs of individual participants. Several members of my team were former Peace Corps members and brought forward the Peace Corps model, which had many lessons to teach but also required customization to apply it to a company and its needs. For one, it could not involve a paid year off, which would make it cost-prohibitive let alone require staff backfill. Rather, the term of such an effort needed to be no more than one month, precluding any need for backfill and avoiding a big tax hit. However, if the work were to be so limited in time, it would need to involve a team assignment, with eight to twelve employees working together. What's more, to justify its existence, it would need to accomplish something tangible not just for the company or its participants, but for society. Teams would need to be multidisciplinary, involving every significant skill represented in the company, from software developers and high-end researchers to business consultants, lawyers, finance people, and marketing experts. Teams also would need to be multicultural, coming from dozens of different countries. Like the Peace Corps, the beneficiaries, who were receiving a team of top talent, would need to be grassroots community organizations in growth markets.

We envisioned a triple benefit. For the company, the model would be a way to recruit new talent, engage existing employees, and provide a high-quality leadership training experience that would develop skills among promising top talent. Also for the company, it would build knowledge and understanding about key growth market geographies. For communities in need, they would receive the equivalent of half a million dollars in targeted consulting services to help them accomplish a major goal. Initially we envisioned selecting 200 top-talent employees a year, on a competitive basis, to participate in what we called Corporate Service Corps.

Creating Corporate Service Corps would require resources in the millions of dollars to be sure, but it would also require partners. Principal among them was an organization called PYXERA Global, a not-for-profit that facilitates mutually beneficial partnerships between the public, private, and social sectors to tackle complex challenges. We invited PYXERA in to meet and discuss how the program would work, seeking not just their participation in designing and making it work, but essentially their agreeing to work cheek by jowl with staff at IBM to fashion assignments that would meet the triple benefit goal.

From concept to launch, Corporate Service Corps was operational in approximately six months, with the initial teams deployed early in 2008. This involved working with constituents on the ground to develop high-quality projects in Asia, Latin America, and Africa. They needed to set lofty goals, but not so lofty that a team assignment could not achieve concrete outcomes. At the same time, top talent within the company needed to be informed about the program, apply for acceptance, be vetted, be assembled into the right teams, and be deployed internationally on a very specific cascade.

The value of this innovative effort can best be described by the project work, the impact on communities in the developing world, the impact on participants, and the impact on IBM. Assignments in Argentina, Colombia, Ecuador, and Mexico procured through the Global FoodBanking Network created a business plan and operations strategy that resulted in a 41 percent increase in food donations, with over 15,000 people fed each month in Toluca, Mexico, alone. In Nigeria, a team working with the government in Cross River State created the management structure for a health care program for poor women and children, serving over 100,000 people in need. In Ethiopia, working with the International Medical Corps, the team helped 46,000 Ethiopians improve their health through improved water, sanitation, and hygiene practices that were outlined and delivered during their engagement. In Peru, the team developed a comprehensive roadmap that allowed a cervical cancer clinic to reach 75,000 women and quadruple its operating income in 2017.

One of the most significant examples was a project, identified by PYXERA and the Peace Corps, focused on dramatically expanding education opportunities for girls and young women in Ghana. Education in Ghana is not equitable by either gender or income. Even for those girls' families who are able to afford the cost of education, far too many have inadequate learning opportunities. The project, under then First Lady Michelle Obama's Let Girls Learn initiative, brought together the Ministry of Education, the Peace Corps, and a local organization called Tech Aid to focus on two core elements. One was to create an enhanced educational opportunity for large numbers of young girls throughout the country, and the second was to expand a mentoring initiative to back up the core education program.

Louise Hemond-Wilson, IBM's chief technology officer for Lab Services, served on a team with expertise in software design, data analytics, and finance. In her day job, Louise heads up a team of 1,100 consultants with a clear focus on emerging markets, but the experience in Ghana gave her the kind of firsthand, on-the-ground experience that could not be matched. The outlined solution was to create a set of learning materials focused on curriculum and life skills provided on an electronic platform accessible on handheld devices or smartphones and through a wireless network. PYXERA offered direct access to the Ministry of Education, and Tech Aid offered access to the wireless network. Peace Corps volunteers on the ground, many teaching in schools, became the conduit to reach large numbers of girls and young women. With the IBM team's multipronged approach, a pilot was developed within months and then ultimately scaled more broadly. According to Louise, the work changed the local attitude not just about this group of business leaders, but about companies in general. Beyond the impact on the community, Louise pointed to the value of the intense learning experience for the team. In the longer term, IBM benefited from enhanced business opportunities in areas unrelated to the work but based on the level of trust established on the ground.

In another project, the team worked in Ho Chi Minh City, Vietnam, to develop a strategy to focus on improvements in water quality.

Over nearly 10 years since the Corporate Service Corps began, 3,000 IBM employees from 60 different geographies were deployed on teams of 8 to 12 people to 37 countries in the developing world. The results of the program were far beyond expectations. Ninety percent of participants said it significantly improved their leadership skills. Ninety-five percent said it improved their cultural awareness, and nearly 80 percent said it boosted their desire to complete their careers at IBM. Roberta Terkowitz, an IBMer from Bethesda, Maryland, said, "It was the most life-altering experience of my life to date, excepting only the birth of my children and not excepting surviving cancer." She participated in a team project in Tanzania.

Over the decade, IBM delivered an estimated over $75 million of pro bono consulting services through more than a thousand critical projects on the ground in countries like Kenya, Cambodia, Ethiopia, and Ghana. For IBM, the program has resulted in improved retention rates for top talent and has become an important component in top talent recruitment worldwide. It has also attracted other companies to follow the IBM model, including J.P. Morgan, Unilever, and Dow Chemical. In fact, over a dozen other companies—many of them IBM clients—have joined IBM teams and understood the benefit of this approach by experiencing it firsthand. J.P. Morgan, in fact, has embraced this approach as a critical component of its citizenship programs and strategies.

Critical to the scale up of this innovation has been the collaboration between IBM and key civil society actors. PYXERA in particular has been very instrumental. PYXERA CEO Deirdre White, a leader in international development with deep and broad expertise in strategies for growth in the developing world, has said that Corporate Service Corps is unique based on its size, scale, and IBM's long-term commitment. She feels that it is incredibly unique that IBM has not only committed to its own program, but has grown the program to include and provide valuable resources to other companies. PYXERA has seen the program grow from one company to more than 20, and from

500 IBMers engaged each year to nearly 3,000 each year across all participating companies.

When the program launched, according to Deirdre, many of the not-for-profits in the developing world with whom PYXERA worked saw the private sector, and especially large global companies, through a decidedly negative lens. They had an attitude that could only be described in the best case as trepidation, and in the worst case as mistrust: "Why are they doing this? What do they expect to get out of it? Do we really need more consultants to tell us what to do?" Yet very soon thereafter, those attitudes changed. Recipient organizations got enormous benefits, not just via the projects that were completed but the skill building that was a core element of what was left behind after engagements were concluded. According to Deirdre, the recipients were supported to learn new and enhanced skills in problem solving and documentation.

Corporate Service Corps is clearly a model for other companies, but it also led to replication internally at IBM with the creation of a Smarter Cities Challenge that focused team projects on assisting cities in their efforts to serve their citizens more effectively, and a Health Corps that focused specifically on ways to assist in innovative health care challenges.

JPMorgan Chase: A Company's Values Are at the Core of Its Actions

The IBM examples are just that, examples. But leadership on the issue of corporate responsibility comes from more than one company and industry.

A noteworthy example is JPMorgan Chase. JPMC, whose founder, J. P. Morgan, was discussed in the previous chapter as someone whose leadership rescued the nation from the danger of a deep recession, has recently embarked upon an effort to invest significantly in targeted and focused ways in cities like Detroit and Chicago. They assist states and localities in strategy and practice to revitalize cities and neighborhoods, improve career and technical education, encourage small business growth, and address the need for a focus on workforce development. The problems in cities where an increasing number of Americans live are not siloed, and are very much interconnected.

Five years ago, according to CEO Jamie Dimon, the company embarked upon a major shift in its efforts to impact more effectively on societal problems. At that time, 40 percent of the company's roughly $200 million in citizenship investments were focused on what the company felt were the four most critical issues: jobs, neighborhood revitalization, small business growth, and financial health. Five years later, under the leadership of Dimon and his global head of Corporate Responsibility, Peter Scher, JPMC remade its strategy and more than doubled that commitment, making 90 percent of its citizenship investment efforts on those four areas. JPMC launched its own Service Corps to focus on the challenges in communities around the world, with dozens of its most skilled employees deployed on team projects in New Orleans, Chicago, Detroit, London, and Johannesburg. According to Dimon, it was "IBM's initiative that inspired us to pursue a program that gives employees the opportunity to apply their business, marketing, and financial know-how to help more effectively solve community challenges while honing their own skills."

But the company's efforts did not stop there. In 2013, JPMC announced a $100 million, five-year initiative focused on aiding the recovery and renaissance of the city of Detroit. Its investment commitment was soon increased and the program went far beyond checkbook philanthropy and used the company's best assets, its lending capacity, and the time and talent of its best people. The focus on small businesses, especially women- and minority-owned businesses, expanded financing opportunities, coupled with technical assistance and support. They also targeted $50 million in community financing to spur broader levels of economic growth. The leadership and commitments made by JPMC attracted three times that amount in additional financing from sources other than JPMC. They also targeted another nearly $30 million in neighborhood revitalization funding for specific projects and approximately $10 million in small business expansion funds, much of it focused on women- and minority-owned businesses but also reaching other small businesses. Over 20 projects were funded, affecting 1,800 small businesses and leading to the creation of over 175,000 square feet of commercial space, much of it in the center of town. The result of this assistance expanded the employment base and saved many more jobs. Based on the success of the program in economic benefits, including job placements, the company committed to replicating the model in the city of Chicago as well, focusing largely on the South Side, with an investment of $50 million focused on a similar network of programs and services. It later announced another $20 million targeted in Washington, D.C. The company also embraced the focus on career and technical education, providing planning and implementation grants to spur a clearer pathway from school to college to career.

As a result of this work, JPMC was ranked number one by *Fortune* magazine in corporate performance in corporate responsibility. And going beyond its citizenship activities, the company made significant commitments in its core operations. It increased its minimum wage, intensified its hiring and promotion of both women and minorities, and continues as a partner in IBM's Corporate Service Corps. According to Jamie Dimon, "JP Morgan began to raise the wages of its U.S. employees to between $12 and $16.50 an hour, something that impacts 18,000 of our bank tellers, customer service representatives, and other employees." The rationale, he outlined, is because "wage stagnation is an important part of the way we can address income inequality."

Starbucks

Starbucks provides another example of a company addressing a critical problem in a very effective fashion. The company's commitment to corporate responsibility owes a good deal to the leadership of its CEO, Howard Schultz. Under Schultz's direction, Starbucks' college achievement plan was launched as a partnership with Arizona State University. It offers Starbucks employees free tuition to obtain their bachelor's degree. However, participation is restricted to employees of Starbucks who work at least 20 hours for the company. Employees who pursue their bachelor's while working at Starbucks receive 42 percent off their Arizona State tuition up front. Over time, in addition to financial aid programs accorded to all students, Starbucks makes up the difference. This not only provides employees with an opportunity, but a built-in incentive to succeed. Importantly, there are few restrictions on the type of degree that the program supports, giving employees wide latitude regarding their career goals, with 60 different degree programs included.

In addition, there is no requirement for students to commit to working for Starbucks for any time period once they've earned their degree.

The core elements of Starbucks' program differ from a number of public tuition support programs, which very often have a range of restrictions built into them, largely in order to obtain political support at the state level. But since this is a private initiative solely supported with company funding, it has built in more flexibility for employees. After the program was announced, it was enriched further; Starbucks employees, who in addition to being interested in pursuing a degree are also U.S. military veterans, have the ability to add one family member to the program, extending the free tuition benefit even further. Again, this is something that would have been difficult to do purely with public funding.

American Express

American Express has chosen to focus a good deal of its attention on building the skill and capacity of the not-for-profit sector overall. As mentioned earlier, a good deal of the delivery of needed services in areas like health care, social services, mental health, education, arts, culture, and science is made neither by the public nor private sectors, but by civil society or the not-for-profit sector. Unlike government and the private sector, the existence of education or human resources programs to build skills across this sector is woefully inadequate. Some graduate schools, some in business schools like Harvard, and others in public policy schools like New York University or Columbia, have focused on creating such programs, some with degrees and others with credentials. Oftentimes the support for these efforts has come from the philanthropic sector. Over the last decade American Express has created and implemented a focused effort to build skills across the not-for-profit sector. In 2008, the American Express Leadership Academy was launched across the United States and globally to address the skills issue across all sectors of civil society, providing pro bono and volunteer services to a range of not-for-profits and donating millions of dollars of needed skill-building and consulting services. American Express's consistent support has built the skills of hundreds of leaders across the sector, and the evaluation results are encouraging, improving skills and managerial abilities. The programs consist of education courses, both online and in person, along with mentoring and other supports. Many foundations, corporations, and even not-for-profit organizations focus on support for civil society, but American Express is unique in the level of support, the consistent length of time that support has been evident, and the structure and outcomes delivered.

The Food Industry

It is not just large companies that are examples of responsible corporate leadership. Chobani, the yogurt company, with actions reminiscent of George Eastman, the founder of Kodak, last year made a commitment to transfer ownership of 10 percent of the company stock to its employees. Chobani, and CEO Hamdi Ulukaya in particular, has distinguished itself for responsible business practices, instituting a high minimum wage and making commitments to the communities where it is located.

Kind, which makes and sells health bars, exhibits strong leadership, mirroring the activities of larger and older companies. Its CEO, Daniel Lubetzky, is the son of a Holocust survivor. Daniel's father was a prisoner in Dachau and came very close to dying of starvation. His story inspired his son and influenced his values and those of his company. Daniel and I worked closely together on an effort to promote peace in the Middle East, providing IBM technological support to obtain consensus and support for a comprehensive solution to tensions in that part of the world. Since becoming CEO of Kind he has coupled the issue of strong business and strong community values and embedded them in the construct of the company.

He made an extraordinary pledge of $5 million, later followed by another $20 million, to set up a not-for-profit to examine health standards for food and nutrition. Rather than spend its money on lawyers and lobbyists, Daniel's effort will have no formal ties to his company. Instead, it will be led and staffed by independent experts, who will develop research and standards for food and nutrition across the industry. The focus on industry standards began for Daniel and Kind when the FDA issued a warning for them to cease using the word "healthy" on their bars. There was an FDA regulation that said snack foods with more than 3 grams of fat cannot use the word on their wrappers. Kind's bars had more than 3 grams of fat, largely because they contained nuts.

While initially taking the word off the wrapper, Kind was determined to do more than that. The company embarked upon an effort to address the issues of food, nutrition, and health standards by filing suit along with leaders in health and nutrition to address the ability to use the word "healthy" under certain circumstances. For example, were one to use avocado or other healthy ingredients in a snack bar, the amount of fat might increase but other health benefits would increase as well. Kind was successful in obtaining this qualification, and this example provides evidence of the way in which the company addresses key societal issues in its product and its commitment to community. Beyond that, it has also addressed issues closer to home by providing some unique benefits to its employees via the Kind Hardship Fund. The fund provides emergency cash assistance to employees who might have a family issue or be faced with a hardship due to disability, illness, or some other difficult circumstance. And while initially open to any of Kind's 650 full- and part-time employees, the fund is also open to those with whom the company works or has a more tangential relationship. For example, a cleaning lady not on Kind's payroll needed cash support for a plane ticket to visit her ailing mother in the Dominican Republic, and the company opened its fund to assist her. Without that assistance she would not have had this opportunity.

Ben & Jerry's, the ice cream company, had a long history as a good corporate citizenship even before it was acquired by Unilever, a global company that prides itself on its strong corporate citizenship profile. Ben & Jerry's initiated a self-imposed fee on greenhouse gas emissions and made investments to ensure that its products did not contain any artificial growth hormones. In addition, it made philanthropic investments in its communities. However, it had been criticized by some for the working conditions of its suppliers, the farm workers who provided the ingredients to make the ice cream. In 2017, Ben & Jerry's created a program called Milk with Dignity, providing employees who work for farms with which it does business, largely migrant workers, at least one day off a week, eight hours of rest between shifts, and access to safe and clean housing, along with compliance with the state minimum wage. An outside entity monitors the program.

Failures in Corporate Citizenship

These are examples where companies across a range of industries, large and small, have gone far beyond simple philanthropy to develop focused models of intervention, deep and constructive partnerships with public- and voluntary-sector institutions, and very importantly have agreed to sustain involvement and investment over time.

And yet, just as more companies are approaching corporate responsibility in a comprehensive and strategic fashion, the examples of bad behavior have clearly not abated. Toyota was confronted with documentation about faulty brake systems, and instead of recalling vehicles, which was dictated, simply added side airbags to its vehicles, the antithesis of a credible and effective response. Chevron, at a time when the standards of environmental behavior are being raised, dumped toxic waste in the rain forests in Ecuador. The United Airlines CEO was forced to resign as a result of unethical dealings with the leadership of the Port Authority of New York and New Jersey, one of 82 CEOs in a five-year period who needed to leave their posts as a consequence of ethical issues. Wells Fargo had to accept responsibility for creating more than 3 million bogus bank accounts, opened in the names of existing customers. Tyco International and the theft crimes committed by its former CEO, Dennis Kozlowski, who subsequently served a prison term, have been widely covered. The media attention focused on Kozlowski and his chief financial officer, Mark Swartz, doctoring their books, defrauding their shareholders, and stealing $150 million. To top it off, they also engaged in illegal and fraudulent environmental practices.

At the end of 2008, Merrill Lynch provided its official filing required in the impending takeover by the Bank of America (as part of a government bailout). The proxy statement, required under law, failed to even mention that in 2009 the company was to distribute nearly $6 billion in employee bonuses for their performance in 2008, a year when the company had operating losses of $28 billion and had already paid out employee bonuses of $3.6 billion. While the 2009 bonuses would normally be paid in January as had always been the practice, the timeline was moved up to December 2008, which was roughly the same time that $25 billion in government funding was provided to Bank of America as part of the bailout arranged in October 2008. The public reaction was outrage. Bank of America said it was unaware of the bonuses and the payout plans. However, this proved to be false. Ultimately, Bank of America and the SEC reached an agreement that the bank would be forced to pay a penalty of $33 million to settle the claim that it intentionally misled the public about its finances.

Many of the companies that have had these difficult experiences have worked hard to correct them and to exert leadership that will limit this kind of activity going forward.

While Enron went out of business and officials from Enron went to jail, many more companies wound up going out of business or paying huge fines for their related bad ethics and scandalous behavior. Arthur Andersen, Enron's auditors and at the time of the Enron scandal one of the "big five" accounting firms, recently spun off its consulting practice, which is now called Accenture. In 2001, Andersen employees systematically destroyed documents to cover up how connected Andersen was to Enron, hiding Enron's fraud and consistently papering over fraudulent accounting practices. Ironically, when Andersen was created in 1913, its founder established the company motto: "Think straight, talk straight." In the five years before Enron blew up, Andersen had paid out more than $500 million to settle lawsuits, and in 2002 a host of its clients had to restate billions in earnings. One of those companies, Waste Management, had to restate its earnings by $1.7 billion.

Negative behavior by companies cannot only be understood by listing the many examples that led to fines or even imprisonment. Silicon Valley companies have been widely criticized for their lack of racial and gender diversity. Except in rare instances, this is not a crime, but on the other hand, it contributes to negative views of companies and contributes to ongoing racial and economic inequality and institutional racism. While some companies have chosen to address this problem via expansion of their scholarship and fellowship programs, others have simply refused to recognize it as a problem at all. Such companies will learn the hard way that these kinds of behaviors are not worth the risk. Sound and effective labor practices, including respect for gender and race, are critical for business to enhance innovation, which has its basis in diversity of perspective, thought, and experiences.

Private-Sector Leadership in the Public and Volunteer Sectors

There are many examples of public-sector leaders who come from the private sector. Some have succeeded; some have not. There are also examples of private-sector leaders who have extended their leadership into civil society, both in serving on the boards of not-for-profit organizations and, in many cases, founding them. In addition, there are examples of corporate and individual philanthropy focused on important societal objectives.

A case in point is New York City's experience with a mayor who, when elected, entered government without any prior government experience. Michael Bloomberg was elected mayor of New York City right after the tragedy of September 11, 2001. His financial independence, combined with his entrepreneurial instincts, impacted city operations. While his tenure was not 100 percent positive, there are several solid examples of where his leadership, honed in the private sector, benefited the city in significant ways. Bloomberg led the ban on smoking in restaurants and bars, which was something that likely would not have been attempted had the mayor needed financial support from those in the private sector who would be negatively affected by such a ban. Bloomberg's financial independence allowed him to do what was right for residents' health regardless of the effect on political contributions.

Perhaps the most important initiative was the mayor's strategy to recruit a top-tier university to partner with the city to develop an innovative technology center on Roosevelt Island. Using the city's assets, real estate, tax policy, and incentives, he sponsored an open competition where universities around the world bid to operate the technology center. Led by his deputy mayor, Bob Steel, who also came from the private sector at Goldman Sachs but also had public-sector experience working in the Treasury Department, and as a board chair of not-for-profit organizations like the After-School Corporation on whose board I also sat, the proposals pledged not only to connect to the technology industry via research and development, but to match the city contributions through fund-raising designed to amass the capital needed to make the project a reality. The project was initially announced in 2011, with the winner chosen in 2013, and the ribbon cutting for the technology center under the aegis of Cornell University took place in the fall of 2017. Could any public official have had the vision for such an initiative and bring it to reality? Of course. However, in this instance, the experience, networks, and connections of Mayor Bloomberg and the understanding of the importance of public-private partnerships all contributed to making this effort come to life. It should be no surprise that many other geographies are looking at this model of attracting businesses and sectors of the business community with a combination of incentives.

The lessons in corporate responsibility are clear. We have seen significant changes as we move into the twenty-first century. Corporate responsibility is a function the importance of which has been significantly increased. Its reporting lines have been upgraded; the work is more professional; and the examples of success and leadership are more prevalent. Core company values and codes of conduct are more explicit. Rating entities have proliferated, and explicit standards or behavior are outlined and expected to be given a rank on those schemes, and have been adopted by governments and other businesses. Socially responsible investors have more influence and more resources, and they have exercised them in significant ways. Business ethics courses have increased in business schools, and other professional schools as well. All of this combined has raised the bar with respect to performance and corporate citizenship. The examples of success, whether IBM, JPMorgan Chase, or American Express, and smaller companies like Chobani or Kind, are noteworthy. Yet examples of bad behavior persist. In some instances, these examples of bad behavior were motivated by greed or lack of ethics. In other cases, it has been a lack of leadership at the top, an absence of core values, or both. The positive examples can be attributed to leadership at the top, core values, and changes in corporate culture coming as a result of the rising composition of millennials in the workforce. And yet the positives and negatives exist concurrently as they always have, and always will.

The results, coupled with the economic changes and challenges, however, have contributed to overall views about the private sector that are negative and ultimately harmful to the country. Society needs strong business engagement on issues like education, the environment, health care, and social services. None of these issues can be addressed by government acting alone. Companies need to engage by contributing their best assets, not just their excess cash via philanthropy. Company policies need to reinforce this. And company practices need to project strong values and strong ethics.

Lessons to Be Learned, and Moving Forward

For companies large and small this starts with adoption and regular reviews and updating of core values. And those values need not only be set at the top, though leadership is important. Employees need to be part of the process of setting and then owning the company values. Those values need to be understood and valued and practiced by the workforce, and that involves an effort to communicate those values consistently for new hires and the existing workforce. A Harvard Business School case written by Professor Rosabeth Moss Kanter outlined the importance of IBM's values and the way in which a deliberate internal communications strategy resulted in employees owning those values.

Next, the company needs to review all of the company's behaviors to ensure they are aligned with those values and make sure that training and support is offered so that employees understand how to bring those values into practice day in and day out, reflecting the differences in geographies as needed. Then a company needs to have a built-in process to examine all of its core practices to make certain they align with its core values. This includes labor practices, environmental stewardship, supply chain practices, governance, and community engagement.

Adopting any set of values will not be effective unless it is coupled with an implementation plan. Regular internal and external reporting is vital to keep those values and practices current and up to date. Finally, there needs to be a structural effort to ensure that the way in which these issues are addressed and practiced is something that is brought to the attention of a company's senior leadership on a regular basis so they can determine ways to go forward.

Of course, the challenge going forward is not to pull away from raising the bar for performance. Quite the contrary, we need to raise the bar even higher. But it is now time to step back and develop and implement far more effective strategies that will dramatically expand the positive examples from strong case examples and models into more effective and scalable strategies that are systemic. This will ensure that strategies are put in place that no longer simply assume that some will achieve high standards, while others will violate the very same ethical standards. What we need is a set of larger-scale structural changes, some of which will need to be built around particular issues, whether labor and employment, education, the environment, and/or economic development, that will accomplish the two critical objectives to move us forward. First, make high-quality activities in corporate responsibility the norm, not the exception. Second, stem the tide of bad ethical behavior by some and as a result engender the strong support of the public. This cannot be accomplished by companies acting alone. We need to accompany this imperative with the ability to work effectively and collaboratively with government, civil society, and among companies. The lessons of the past and the successes and failures in the present dictate that we take a more comprehensive approach as we move forward.

The next step is the future.

Chapter 3

The Future

The history of corporate responsibility and a review of where it currently stands provide us with important background and context for its future direction. The facts I've presented in the book ought to dispel a good deal of the simplistic and undocumented view that all corporate behavior is and always has been bad. It has not been, is not, and will not be going forward. As in all sectors of society—business and industry, government, and civil society—there are examples of good and bad behavior. A review of history and the present also tells us that the most exemplary behavior by the private sector has been proactive rather than reactive to either law or regulation. This is not to say that regulation is ineffective in setting standards and addressing problematic behavior, but in terms of preventing such behavior, and more important in stimulating higher levels of performance and real leadership, it is not the only solution, and perhaps not even the solution of choice. This is instructive and hopefully clarifies some assumptions about corporate behavior. But most important, it can provide us an opportunity based on an understanding of fact, to provide a road map for a future that is not made up of good and bad actors. We need to do better, much better. The question is, where do we want to be? And how can we get there?

For more than 100 years we have seen some companies exhibit extremely bad behavior at the same time that others have done just the opposite. Across industries and across segments of the business community, we have always seen companies and their products come and go. Many of the most successful companies and industries in each decade over the last century have bitten the dust. Bad ethical behavior is certainly not the only reason that companies fail, though it is clear it can be a contributing factor. At the same time, other companies and some entire industries have continued to successfully reinvent themselves. As companies reinvent and innovate, a strong company code of conduct and strong ethical guidelines are not the only reasons why they are able to survive and grow, but are definitely contributory factors. Enron and WorldCom and so many others are no longer in business today, while others like Volkswagen and Wells Fargo have paid a price for their transgressions and are attempting to put extensive effort into attempting to reverse and make up for the behavior that exposed them to such justifiable criticism. Some regulatory measures have been successful in convicting after the fact those whose business behavior was unethical. But the examples of good practices and leading practices of iconic companies like American Express, IBM, and J.P. Morgan, along with newer companies like Starbucks, Chobani, and Kind, are just as important to understand. None of these companies are perfect, but they demonstrate a commitment to the positive role that business can play in society. It's a commitment built into the company ethos and promoted and emphasized by the leadership. Their products and business models have undergone and will continue to undergo dramatic changes, and their leadership on societal issues has evolved and will evolve as well.

The commitment to core values in the case of these companies and many others has stayed constant, and perhaps is the reason why they have endured. A lack of strong values and ethics contributes to the bad behavior of those whose names are symbols of what corporate responsibility should not be.

The problems facing our nation today are in some cases quite similar to or a continuation of those the nation has grappled with in years and decades past, though in some cases they have evolved to some degree and the barriers to change have perhaps become more formidable: How to convert unemployment and wage stagnation into job growth. How to ensure both economic and social stability to ensure success for all regardless of geography, race/ethnicity, or gender. How to deal with environmental risk and create environmental reward and stability. How to address the challenge of creating and sustaining effective and productive education and health systems. How to put in place an effective social safety net for those at the bottom of the pyramid. How to address the challenges of immigration, continued racial, ethnic, and gender discrimination and divisions, and of course the issue of income inequality. While these problems and challenges are more nuanced than they may have appeared ten and even a hundred years ago, they remain perhaps the most significant challenges facing all of us in society today, across all sectors of the economy, and they are desperately in need of comprehensive solutions. None of these problems can be addressed by any one sector of society on its own, or by any one business, or any layer of government operating alone. Complex problems require cross-sector collaboration in order to achieve meaningful change.

Depending on their political persuasion, some see the solutions on the left, while others see them on the right. But hopefully all agree that government at all levels—local, state, and federal—must play a significant role in addressing national challenges. Some would see it in the level of funding allocated to address an issue, or the level of taxation or regulation imposed by government. However, while governmental action and initiative can and must play an important role, it cannot possibly address these challenges on its own. Assistance is crucial from civil society and the private sector. Can government address the challenge of finding a cure for cancer by excluding the range of major not-for-profit players like the American Cancer Society? Can government alone address the ability to respond to natural disasters without the cadre of critical first responders like the Red Cross, Doctors Without Borders, or the International Rescue Committee? Can government address the challenges of social services, mental health, or substance abuse without working with civil society and the key not-for-profit social service providers who are on the front lines serving the millions of Americans in need of assistance? Of course not. While government is a major funder and regulator of all of these activities, the expertise and the delivery of service comes largely from civil society, with added support from the private and philanthropic sector. The resources and authority to act may be different across the key constituencies, but the reality is that government and civil society must work in close partnership and collaboration along with the private sector to effectively address any of these issues. With respect to government stimulating job growth or tackling the skills crisis, is this possible without the employers, large and small, who need people with the right skills or the companies whose innovation will drive economic growth? Without a doubt the answer is no.

The next and most logical question is how does the private sector fit into the equation. What role can they play in close partnership with government and civil society, and with other companies within and outside of their sector? Do they simply resemble private foundations or individuals of significant wealth, who donate some of their excess cash, with tax incentives to do so, largely functioning simply as another funding mechanism? Or should they be more than that? Can they be a collaborator or perhaps even a leader and innovator? And can they mobilize and contribute more than just their excess cash, not forgoing cash donations, but focusing instead on their most valuable assets—innovation and human resources? And beyond financial and other resources, can they live up to a significantly higher ethical standard of behavior and operate their companies in a way that will not only justify the support of their employees, shareholders, and customers, but provide a marked financial return to the company and society over the long run?

Do we as a society expect companies, their leaders along with their executives and employees, at a bare minimum to live up to a high ethical standard of behavior in the way they conduct themselves? Can we and should we expect more? Should companies live up to high environmental standards and strong labor practices? Should they have a responsibility to the communities where they live, work, and do business as leaders? Can they speak out in favor of or in opposition to certain policies that could negatively affect not just one company but communities as well? And most important, should they have an obligation to exert leadership within the business community and beyond in addressing all of these challenges in a collaborative fashion, speaking out publicly when the need arises, and using their economic influence and their innovative spirit to contribute to effective solutions to the most pressing challenges facing the world today?

If we raise the bar—and clearly we need to do so—can the raised bar be cleared, then raised again? And how can this best be done, and what will be the accrued benefit for those who do so and the consequences for those who do not?

I've posed a lot of questions. But all are necessary and worthy of consideration. And they need to be asked, re-asked, and asked again. Efforts such as this require frequent and ongoing review, and honest assessments, to keep moving forward.

Building upon the past and the present, the future now provides us with an opportunity to move beyond the good and bad actors and break the mold of the last hundred-plus years of having good players and bad players in the private sector. We now have an opportunity to go beyond mere standards of behavior or rating schemes that target or praise actors in the private sector for examples of success. We now have an opportunity for many, not just some, to exert real leadership in partnership with government and civil society, with the result being a more problem-free society leading to greater economic success, equity, and equality across our nation.

Importantly, the future is now. We need not wait decades or even years to start the clock on a brighter future. The future is now.

Let start with a focus on leadership and ethics.

Leadership: We Need Leaders to Lead

The business community has in the past frequently chosen to engage on public policy issues of concern to society. With respect to education, there has been strong support within the business community in the United States for education reform from the late 1980s into the early part of the twenty-first century. There have also been concrete actions in support of racial diversity going back to the middle of the twentieth century. Companies took the lead in their labor practices and community engagement, in many cases ahead of government action. In the current time frame, we have seen many companies come out in favor of addressing the challenge of climate change through their corporate practices, but also speaking out publicly in favor of policy as well as practice. Others have led the focus on infrastructure, immigration reform, and workforce issues. And while individual business leaders have spoken out on these and other issues and have used their philanthropic programs to support programs and organizations active in these areas, with some important exceptions, like the efforts of former New York City mayor and business leader Michael Bloomberg on the issues of climate change, and gun control, they have more frequently involved themselves in economic issues such as trade and tax than on broader societal issues. And most of the coordinated advocacy on these issues has been pursued individually rather than corporately through their membership on the boards of certain organizations or via their personal philanthropy, or in positions taken by business or trade associations representing purely business interests.

As we move into the future it is important for leaders in the private sector to speak out more forcefully, more consistently, and publicly on critical issues concerning society as a whole, and to do so in an organized and coordinated fashion. Most business associations and industry groups are put together to advance business growth and guard against actions by government that might harm them. There are few, if any, organizations created with the express purpose of providing a coherent voice representing businesses' views on a range of key societal issues. Very often we have seen government leaders at the local, state, and national levels convene business leaders and ask for commitments to move forward on a particular policy issue. A clear example of the success of that type of action was the leadership demonstrated by President John F. Kennedy in asking companies to make commitments to address the lack of African Americans in their workforce by altering their hiring practices. Subsequently, nearly every U.S. president has convened business leadership to ask them to make commitments to address a key issue. For instance, President Obama did it to ask for commitments on immigration issues. Clearly, in the case of President Kennedy and President Obama, this resulted in some progress, though not nearly enough, and it did result in action and change. But business leadership needs to be out in front of being required by a government leader to make and then meet commitments, and it needs to be far-reaching, proactive, and coordinated.

While there will continue to be evidence of such actions, without a change in approach, we can expect it to be tied to a newly elected leader and specific to one concern. However, there is no high-profile, organized, and concerted effort to do this on a national level beyond pure business-related issues and involving a set of high ethical business standards and leadership focused on a deep and concrete way for business to address critical societal issues. There are examples of governmental task forces or committees that have been created with business involvement, and the same is true in civil society, but there is no long-term multi-issue organization with strong business leadership partnered with government and key leadership from civil society for the express purpose of analyzing key societal issues and forcefully advocating for systemic shared solutions, and doing so in a nonpolitical fashion. This vacuum is something that needs to be filled in order to demonstrate the strength of business as an advocate for addressing key societal issues, done in a thoughtful way, with multisector engagement, goals, and objectives, and metrics and measurements to assess and evaluate progress toward achieving desired outcomes.

There are key issues facing society: the social safety net for those at the bottom; climate change and its effect on stability; education. Even issues like immigration and gun safety would benefit from concerted business leadership. Many of these issues are interconnected and, truthfully, can only be addressed in a coordinated fashion. For example, the push for education standards connects directly to economic growth and opportunities, as does a focus on immigration and diversity. This type of organization demonstrating cross-sector leadership needs to be created.

We have seen enormous leadership from the business community on the issue of philanthropy where extremely wealthy individuals—Warren Buffett and Bill Gates, for example—have modeled a pledge to get other individuals of great wealth to make commitments to donate significant amounts of money through personal philanthropy. This is very much needed and appreciated. We have also seen business leaders like Mike Bloomberg assume leadership on key environmental issues or the problems within cities, but this needs to go beyond the leadership of individuals in the business community and must lead to more concerted attention across the private sector.

What is needed is a high-level, highly visible, new and totally independent organization—not a trade association and not a membership group, but an organization that will set goals and objectives and organize and achieve progress across sectors on the key societal issues and also on ethical behavior. It should be clear to everyone that business needs to play a positive role in affecting those issues that impact on society: education, economic development, health care, the environment, and more, and leadership from the sector as a whole on such issues is essential. There is no legislative or regulatory barrier to doing this. It would not involve a huge cost or a significant risk. It simply needs the leadership, political will, and participation of high-profile business leaders who would work together to create and lead it and make sure it does not address the narrow concerns of business, or one sector of the business community, but instead the shared concerns of all areas of society.

Ethics and Community Service: A Culture of Ethics and Service Needs to Be Reinforced and Expanded

If we examine carefully both historically and into the present the examples of good and bad behavior, it all seems to come down to ethics, standards of behavior, and values. Do people in the private sector have a strong sense of ethics and a core set of values that connect both to being good and to doing good, or don't they? And importantly, are those ethical standards communicated and supported up and down the organization, connected to training, compensation, and promotions? Many companies have statements about corporate values and beliefs, but many do not. And many others, in addition to such statements, ask or require all of their employees to participate in ethics training. But again, many do not. Some actually require their employees to sign a statement annually accepting strong ethical values and making those standards of behavior clear, and then holding their workforce accountable for their performance; many other companies back it up with sanctions and rewards specifically related to those behaviors. Some connect it to promotion and compensation. But again, most companies do not. Companies that are in the lead in these activities ought to set the standard for others and have those standards met or exceeded by many.

However, in spite of these practices that are demonstrations of taking the issue of business ethics seriously, the bar needs to be raised, and raised significantly. As we head into the future it is important that all, and not just some, companies replicate best practices in this regard. All companies need to embrace strong ethical behavior as part of their company work experience and standards. All companies need to provide training and support to not just be aware of the importance of ethical practice, but also to engage in them. And all companies need to have their employees go through a yearly process of understanding and then formally agreeing to conduct themselves according to such clear standards of behavior. This is something that businesses can do on their own. But it cannot stop there.

City, state, and national Chambers of Commerce need to make these kinds of activities part of their requirements for membership, and they need to provide advice and support toward their members' ability to comply with such standards. And this can't only happen at the national level. State and local associations need to adopt the same practice. Ethical standards, practices, and behavior need to be adopted as a core set of standard practices across businesses, and those who comply need to be recognized, while those who do not need to be singled out for improvement and offered help to do better.

There is also a need to follow through on actions to make ethics a clearer and stronger element in education at all levels—from elementary through higher education—so that everyone is better prepared to enter into the workforce with an understanding and appreciation of the importance of defined values and ethics. Decades ago business schools and professional schools began adding optional courses on ethics to their curriculum. While this is admirable, it is hardly enough. Ethical practices and standards need to be part of how a strong academic education is delivered at all levels of education. In business schools this will mean going beyond one optional course and incorporating ethics into courses on finance, marketing, advertising, and communications. In law schools, medical schools, and other professional schools, the effort should be consistently and comprehensively delivered as well. This should be true also in all undergraduate education as well as in high school, middle school, and elementary school. This does not mean a change in curriculum, but simply a change in how the curriculum is taught to stress and then reinforce the importance of ethical behavior in work and life. If we are serious about high-quality education and high-quality work ethics in any and all sectors of the economy, and the private sector in particular, ethics cannot be optional. It needs to be a requirement.

Ethics and civics also need to be a part of how we prepare our teachers to teach. Teachers are under enormous pressure, and are often underpaid, underappreciated, and seldom provided with the professional development they need. As a matter of policy this needs to be addressed, but preparing our teachers to stress citizenship and ethics is also important. Classroom management and curriculum are critically important in building teacher skills. But ethics and civics can't be left merely to on-the-job training. The teaching of ethics is perhaps more important than any other subject, and it doesn't need a license; it needs to be part of every element of teacher preparation and classroom instruction.

Beyond stressing ethics in the classroom, it needs to be learned and reinforced via practice. This can best be addressed via a commitment to citizenship played out through community service. This would bring issues of ethics home in a very real way. Since the launch of the Peace Corps in the 1960s, followed by VISTA, there has been significant interest by some in making community service a much larger part of both policy and practice. Participation in the Peace Corps, VISTA, and other forms of voluntary community service benefits individuals in concrete ways, contributes to community stability, and reinforces ethical conduct. Some have long advocated for a significant expansion of such programs, advocating for a community service requirement, similar to military service, in which service would not be optional. A national service requirement has been advocated by many. A current effort led by General Stanley McChrystal, John Bridgeland, former domestic policy advisor to President Bush, and others, and supported by a bipartisan set of leaders from all sectors of the economy, is making progress. But this effort, and many preceding it that have argued that all Americans should be required to devote some time to community service, has yet to result in the required change in national policy. Some not-for-profit entities have been formed that are committed to assisting young people by providing a year of service through organizations like City Year in but one positive example.

Many of these efforts are also nonpartisan, and they deserve broader support. Connecting the issue of community service to corporate responsibility and ethics can perhaps provide community service with an even stronger rationale.

A commitment to national service is something that would unite the nation across sectors of the economy, and it deserves even broader support. Building on the legacy of the Peace Corps, the early 1990s saw the creation of the Corporation for National Service under the Clinton administration. Although it has not been expanded significantly and has been subject to the whim of budgetary back-and-forths, it was a demonstration of the support for such efforts. Service benefits us all, and is connected to the issues of ethics and values because it offers a practical example of how ethics can be demonstrated, and it ought not be separate from military service or the educational experience. It needs to touch larger and larger numbers of Americans, not the small fraction it does now. Just like ethics, community service ought to be part of how we teach and how we educate, not a separate component.

There has been great interest of late in what educators call project-based learning, meaning that the learning experience can be advanced by connecting students with an educational concept through a practical exercise. Community service and ethics can be joined together in how project-based learning is actually delivered, melding academics with service to provide that practical experience in a way that benefits communities.

By coupling service with academics, we can stress the importance of problem solving, writing, teamwork, and performance metrics. Like embedding ethics in all levels of the education experience, embedding community service in schools and the entire education experience will reinforce the importance of ethical values. And service can demonstrate how they are intertwined. Were we to do this, and also make sure that the bipartisan interest in community service is translated into renewed support for the Corporation for National Service and service for all, over the long term we would reduce bad ethical behavior that ultimately leads to scandal.

At the university level, experiential learning needs to be embraced as well. It can and should be connected to academics and made credit-bearing.

New York governor Andrew Cuomo urged the state university system of New York to make experiential learning a routine part of the educational experience for all students. The state's 60-plus college campuses have made some significant headway in response, but this is something that needs to be embraced not just by one campus or one system or one state; it needs to be implemented nationwide.

The message to the private sector is clear: were companies to take up the mantle upon employment and make ethics and service part of their onboarding for all employees, and then reinforce it through workforce development and ongoing skill building as a core element of their operations, including embedding the practice of values and ethics into employee compensation and promotion systems, those practices and models or behavior would be more likely to become standard practice. Again, this is a recommendation that does not necessarily require an act of Congress, does not require a budget-breaking, large-scale federal appropriation or regulatory changes.

It simply can be done, if we have the leadership and the will to get it done. If we take nothing else away from the lessons of the past and present, it is the importance of leadership and actions that will improve our ethical practices. In years past the private sector was the exemplar in many cases that led others to follow. This can be and should be the case again.

Finally, corporations should not leave standards of behavior to others. Leaders in the private sector need to create their own high standards and metrics of performance and hold themselves responsible for meeting or exceeding them. It was the private sector that shaped how they ought to be held accountable for their financial performance; the same ought to be true of corporate responsibility. Done effectively and with involvement of experts across sectors, it could lead to higher standards and higher levels of achievement.

Key Problems Facing Society Today and How They Can Be Addressed

Leadership commitment and support for a focus on ethics and corporate responsibility is a needed and necessary first step, but the next step is to outline what specifically can be accomplished, and how, in service of those higher standards.

Let's start with the how. As we look at the actions and results of the private sector as it attempts to address critical societal challenges, as we see from past and present efforts, there are ample examples of strong and pathbreaking efforts to address education, skills, labor practices, diversity and inclusion, and the environment. Virtually all of these efforts were initiated by leadership companies, and were initiated at the nexus between a company's business strategy and its commitment to values and ethics. At the same time, when we look at negative business practices, sometimes they were inhibited or reduced by legislative or regulatory practices, in order to eliminate or reduce the risk of incurring financial penalties or a negative effect on a company's brand.

Oftentimes there were incentives to encourage the positive behavior of the private sector. In philanthropy, as one example, the Internal Revenue Service provides a tax incentive to companies, as it does to individuals, if they choose to make financial contributions to eligible not-for-profit organizations. To build upon this, in the age of the personal computer, Congress provided an incentive to companies that contributed computer technology to eligible not-for-profit organizations and education organizations by allowing the tax deduction to be equal to the midrange between the cost and market value of the technology donated. This wound up increasing markedly the amount of technology that was donated, especially to not-for-profits and educational institutions.

In another example, when companies instituted health insurance benefits for their employees, there was a tax incentive to do so. However, incentives—and they need not be restricted to tax incentives alone—do not include the range of labor practices and training opportunities that might address changes in the workforce and the need to keep more people employed. And with respect to philanthropic donations, they have included cash and product donations, whether to a symphony orchestra or to a museum, but they haven't included any incentives for the value of pro bono services designed to impact societal problems. If a company contributes $1 million to a host of not-for-profit organizations, the tax benefit is quantifiable. Yet pro bono services such as responding to natural disasters with "boots on the ground" or addressing cures for cancer or AIDS via the contribution of top-tier researchers or technology advances, provide significant societal benefit but no financial benefit at all to the donor.

Many company employees volunteer on their own time, and some companies match their volunteer time with a cash donation, which is eligible for a tax benefit. This is fine, but it serves to access only a limited amount of the time and talent that might be mobilized. Actually deploying the massive expertise that the private sector has in order to address critical problems facing society results in no financial incentive to the company whatsoever. Clearly this ought to change.

Perhaps companies ought to be incentivized to allow their employees to donate significant amounts of their time on problem-solving activities with not-for-profit organizations and schools. Perhaps they ought to be provided an incentive to allow contractors, and potentially vendors, to participate in their health plans. Perhaps companies that retrain and reskill their employees ought to get an incentive or benefit as well. Perhaps the cost of tuition reimbursement for additional education ought also to be matched with an incentive. These are all ideas that need to be explored, structured, and acted upon in the future. Cost sharing, especially tied to specific positive and measurable outcomes that have a cost savings or cost avoidance component, would go beyond cash donations and encourage more effective business conduct with a real measurable effect on society.

This also ought to include actions that address the challenge of environmental safety, especially climate change. Most legislation and regulation in the area of environmental action provides penalties for bad acts, but few incentives exist for adopting goals and objectives with rewards for performance in ways that reduce a company's carbon footprint or engage its employees in environmental actions with specific and concrete results. Leadership actions that companies take to reduce their carbon footprint ought to be encouraged and then rewarded. Especially when they exceed goals.

Actions by companies to encourage their employees to engage in actions that are positive for the environment ought also be rewarded as well. And this ought not to begin or end with single companies, but should be extended to their supply chains as well. This could include a range of energy-saving activities, including the embrace of solar energy.

As we look to the future, it is time that we reassess the incentives and disincentives not just to do something but to do it well and to reach a high level of performance. And what is done need not only be rewarded with financial incentives. Recognition is incentive enough for many in the private sector, especially if it involves employee leadership. But the focus should be on outcomes and not only process, encouraging a result that impacts positively on societal challenges and builds a more effective and balanced economy. And just as important, we need to move forward in a collaborative fashion.

Here are some concrete examples of things that could easily be done, with concrete benefits to society that build on what is currently taking place across the United States.

First of all, the P-TECH program outlined in the preceding chapter, started by IBM and now embraced by more than 400 other companies and government and education leadership, is a model for career and technical education, and the grades 9–12 structural model needs to be embraced across the United States, ensuring that more students are college-ready and more students complete college as a ticket to a stable career. Businesses large and small across the United States need to participate. The engagement of business directly in education along the lines of the P-TECH design has already proven to have concrete and lasting results for students and for the economy.

Eliminating the need for costly remediation education will allow the savings to be dedicated to enhanced instruction. And most important, improved college completion rates will create added tax benefits and savings of social services costs. This can and should be done with all possible speed, involving thousands of schools, millions of students, and thousands of companies. When we have something that works in education, we need to bring it to scale and make it sustainable. Seeing career and technical education as separate from high-quality academics is the wrong path for our nation. All students need an opportunity to combine strong academics as part of a pathway from school to college to career.

Second, the model of the IBM Corporate Service Corps, embraced by dozens of other companies, needs to spread to not dozens more but to hundreds and hundreds of additional U.S. businesses, large, small, and midsized. Foreign aid and international development funding should not be cut by the federal government, it ought to be enhanced. It creates a more stable global society, but matched with on-the-ground support by teams of private-sector problem solvers it can magnify the results. A program like Corporate Service Corps increases the number of highly skilled businesspeople who can promote, via team projects in the developing world, economic stability and progress and change how people in emerging geographies view the private sector and U.S. companies overall. It will also enhance the knowledge and experience of the next generation of business leaders about the global economy, the need for cultural understanding, and the importance of ethics and community service as essential, not "nice to have." If the Fortune 500 companies had a modest incentive to send at least one hundred of their top people on corporate service teams across the developing world with the goal of stabilizing and growing local economies as a consequence of those economies gaining access to top business leaders with skills in technology, finance, law, marketing, and communications, it would produce significant benefits to companies and their next generation of leaders, giving them important skills and experiences that would make them more effective. Importantly, this type of effort will improve the global landscape. It could focus on critical issues like food and nutrition, environmental safety, disaster preparedness, and job creation. But the range of important resources represented across the private sector ought not be provided solely to international or growth-market geographies. Many companies currently provide some level of pro bono services locally and nationally, and several not-for-profit organizations encourage and coordinate such activities, but unlike with cash donations, they receive no encouragement. This needs to change.

Third, the model of J.P. Morgan's large-scale collaborative activities in cities like Detroit and Chicago needs to be embraced by hundreds of other companies. And it ought not be restricted to financial services companies, offering easy-to-access capital for small business growth and development, but also be expanded to training and technical assistance connected to a city's economic growth and stability. But it cannot and should not begin and end there. We need new strategies and new programs, delivered in a shared cross-sector fashion, to address key societal challenges facing our cities, thus providing cities and their leaders access to the kind of skills and resources that will help them grow and develop.

Cities need assistance in a host of areas, and many, if not most, connect to private-sector skills. Finance, technology, marketing, human resources, and communications are all areas where companies and their employees have significant skills. They match up with areas where cities have significant needs, and the J.P. Morgan approach of focused and targeted multiskill assistance is a model that needs to be embraced and expanded.

Fourth, the action and leadership of American Express's efforts to improve the skills and leadership of the not-for-profit sector needs considerably more attention. Not-for-profit organizations are on the front lines of the creation and maintenance of the social safety net in but one example. Their actions benefit those who need their services, but also benefit all of us because failure to effectively meet this challenge winds up creating risk for every one of us. Most not-for-profit organizations need access to the kind of skill-building support, mentoring, and other services that is common in the private sector. As companies organize their efforts to build the skills of their employees, it would be feasible for them to allocate a fixed set of slots in their training and education programs and make them available to staff and leadership at not-for-profit organizations to improve their skills and impact positively on the populations they serve. This can also extend to service on not-for-profit boards. Many leaders in the private sector build broad service into their work lives, but extending that to the next generation of leaders ought to be incentivized as well.

But we need to do more. Much more. And it is not just what we do, but how we do it.

Critical Issues That Need a New Focus: Education and Jobs

Every year, it seems, surveys are done by major media outlets, whether the *New York Times*, NBC, or ABC, think tanks or academic journals, identifying the year's most pressing problems. Over the last decade a review of literally hundreds of such surveys and policy-oriented publications reveals that while there are some differences in what is on or off each list, based on the year or month the results were released, there are more similarities than there are differences when Americans of all income levels, races, ages, and geographies are asked to identify the most pressing problems facing society today. The same is true when domain experts are asked their view of the problems and how to rank them. And while some are outlined as problems, like lack of trust or understanding, or an unwillingness to work together, many more times the problems are outlined with specificity, such as health care, education, social services, joblessness, the opioid crisis, violence, climate change, immigration, or terrorism. While some lists rank some of these issues higher or lower, the similarities from year to year are striking.

This brings us to perhaps the most critical question of all. How can we address these issues or problems in an innovative fashion so that we can track progress? What is needed are a few big ideas to start with, but the ideas need to be practical, achievable, measurable, and, most important, possible. Achievement needs to be assessed with clear metrics for performance. The results need to be released, socialized, and transparent. Based on outcomes, the efforts need to continue, with modifications and improvements where necessary. Let's start with ways to improve education.

Four Ideas That Will Boost Education Achievement

Public education has four critical challenges that might be addressed were we to reshape the opportunities for innovative actions as a consequence of innovative public-private partnership. The first is the challenge of America's teacher shortage, especially in areas connected to STEM education. The second connects directly to the need to more effectively connect school to career and enhance student opportunities. The third addresses the financial needs our schools face and the significant cost savings that could be made and then plowed into enhanced student services and resulting student achievement. The fourth and perhaps most important are efforts in the private sector, in particular, that will support the work of educators across the nation to focus on educational excellence.

The Teaching Crisis

There are nearly 4 million teachers in America who have the responsibility for educating the 50 million students in K–12 public schools. While the student population is expected to grow by 3 million students over the next decade, the education system is threatened by severe and increasing teacher shortages. Data demonstrate that by 2018 we will see a shortage of over 100,000 teachers nationwide, and the numbers suggest the problem is getting worse, not better. And the prospects going forward show that this is just the tip of the iceberg.

Enrollment in teacher education programs has declined by 35 percent over the last three years. And while the overall teacher shortage problem is severe, it is even worse in areas connected to STEM. Data show that 42 percent of states say there is a shortage of math teachers, and 42 percent of states are facing a shortage of science teachers. It is clear that over the next decade America will need at least 10,000 new science and math teachers. We will have to face the fact that the United States must address this critical teacher shortage via some innovative and creative ways or else we will all pay the price.

The traditional way of addressing a crisis like this is to encourage more Americans to pursue a teaching career. This can be done by providing tuition incentives for those who pursue a teaching career, and offering higher salaries and improved benefits for those who enter and stay in the teaching profession. It is likely that states and the federal government need to move forward with efforts that address the crisis in all of these traditional ways. However, the financial cost of moving forward in this fashion is high, and even if we are willing to pay the price, and we should, it would take time to put such efforts into motion, and requires political will and leadership. What America needs to embrace is a quicker and less expensive approach involving public-private collaboration, which we can endorse and put into place at the same time as we are putting other longer-term efforts into place.

In 2007, IBM began a pilot program called Transition to Teaching. It addressed in a small way the need to find more teachers, especially those interested and skilled to teach math and science. For employees who were approaching retirement and interested in an "encore" career as a teacher, the company provided up to $15,000 per employee to pay the cost of added education courses and practice teaching in order to successfully transition from a career in science and engineering into a second career as a teacher. The program successfully allowed 100 employees to complete the program and become classroom teachers. Their retention rates are high, as is their performance. The program has been successful in making the transition work, meeting the needs of school districts, and doing so quickly, effectively, and economically. This modest example allows us to move forward in a more effective and transformative fashion, bringing this modest example to scale in a way that can provide the maximum benefit.

Concurrent with IBM's activities, a civil society organization called Encore.org created collaborations and partnerships with many companies to encourage their executives and managers seeking a second or encore career to consider the not-for-profit sector as an important opportunity. The level of interest has been considerable.

Since that time the number of skilled Americans in the workforce, especially in areas connected to STEM education, has grown exponentially, and while the average age of workers in the field has lowered, the number at or near traditional retirement ages is increasing.

Currently the size of the U.S. workforce is 158 million. Of that number, about 5 percent, or approximately 8 million, work in science and engineering jobs. And of that number the share of the workforce age 55 and over represents about 20 percent of the total, or 1.6 million. Of course, there are Americans in other professions who are also over 55 and are skilled in science and math as well. The size of the potential skilled population over 55 in this area alone is in excess of 2.5 million.

Data tell us that some of the individuals in these occupations want a traditional retirement, while still others would like to stay in their jobs until their midsixties or later. However, again according to survey data, a majority of them would like to pursue a second career. And of that number, some would be interested in a second career as a teacher. That number could approach 100,000. However, figuring out how to make such a transition happen is daunting, and if we do nothing differently, few will actually wind up in the classroom.

Imagine if we were able to interest, and then train, prepare, deploy, and support, only 15 percent of those science and engineering workers as they consider and then move into encore careers as math or science teachers. This could provide as many as 15,000 new science and math teachers to American schools every year, dramatically and effectively addressing the nation's teaching crisis. Perhaps a thousand of them might be experienced and capable of teaching computer science and training and supporting other teachers to incorporate computer science and technology overall into their instruction in our schools. At the end of only two years the number of new science and math teachers could approach or exceed 30,000, with a potential tenure of five to seven years or more each. Were we to handle teacher preparation, education, and support only via traditional means, the solution would be far more costly, would take a lot more time, and would not bring into teaching a cadre of teachers with broader skills and experiences. If this problem were approached as a combined goal of the private and public sectors, the solution might be implemented promptly, with the benefits accruing to us all. A total cost of $150 million split evenly between public, private, and philanthropic sources could generate 15,000 teachers with a return on investment and cost savings far, far greater than that.

An innovative and effective public-private partnership among the private sector, the public sector, the education sector (elementary, secondary, and higher education), along with needed and necessary support from civil society and philanthropy, could in fact make this all happen. With a minimal amount of shared resources provided by companies as a retirement benefit, coupled with support for training and education provided by government, America could identify, train, prepare, and support enough talent coming from the private sector with top-tier science and engineering skills that would positively impact the educational needs of the next generation and go a long way toward addressing the skills gap facing the nation.

We would need to start with what it would take to encourage one out of a hundred of these workers who are approaching retirement to consider a transition to an encore career as a teacher. We could begin with some tools and techniques the private sector knows well, gathering data and insights about what the target population would need and marketing to them. Working with key business associations, like the Conference Board, the U.S. Chamber of Commerce, and the Business Roundtable, there would need to be surveys of employees in these occupations to determine what it would take for them to pursue such a second career option. Second, to provide more granularity and make the survey data more useful as a jumping-off point, there would need to be sessions with prospective candidates in groups to determine their preferences for the types of preparation, coursework, mentor support, and added online support. This ought to be done in concert with teachers to make it effective. Concurrently, working with the National Council Chief State School Offices (CCSSO), the National School Boards Association, leading schools of education, along with teachers' and principals' associations, there would need to be a profile of the balance between courses, practice teaching, mentor support, and professional development needed to best prepare and support these candidates and an alignment with the geographies that would most benefit. This could be done on a state-by-state level. In this work there would also be opportunities for support and collaboration with civil society, especially those organizations like Encore.org that have established track records in this space in identifying and engaging people interested in encore careers. An entity, likely a public-private partnership, would then assume responsibility for coordinating and launching this effort, with clear benchmarks and metrics for evaluating success, modifying, and then improving the work.

When we examine any potential solution, the term "win-win" often captures the solutions that need our full engagement and support. This effort, which is achievable and cost-effective, can be described as a "win-win-win." The first win would provide the needed teaching resources our children and our schools desperately need to move STEM education forward, and do so in a cost-effective manner. The second win would move a significant number of older workers out of their current jobs but do so in a less disruptive, less expensive, and more planned way. The third win would open up new opportunities for a cohort who would fill the jobs that become vacant, providing employment opportunities that would enrich their lives and improve competitiveness.

This could not be achieved by government or education institutions operating alone, or by business operating alone. But if embraced as an achievable long-term, multisector strategy, it could provide an important pillar upon which to build success addressing the teacher shortage.

Development of Schools and Education as a Makerspace

Many school buildings across the United States are only partially occupied. Vacancy rates vary by state, city, and district, but are particularly significant in cities like Chicago, Detroit, and Pittsburgh, as well as in smaller geographies, both urban and rural. Higher education institutions have historically been very aggressive in seeking private companies to locate in spaces within their institutions in order to advance a research agenda and engage in collaborative entrepreneurial activities, which typically result in a range of public-private partnerships. By doing so, colleges have accessed the benefits in opportunities for students and faculty, along with resource partnerships that benefit participating institutions. Shared resource partnerships have generated intellectual capital and a range of broader economic opportunities. This has not been the case in K–12. However, were vacant space in school buildings to be made available to companies, both start-ups and established companies, there could be significant benefits for all participants, from government, to business, to the education sector, to civil society.

Public school buildings that are only partially occupied and have vacant classrooms offer potential access after school hours to athletic facilities, auditoriums, cafeterias, libraries, and other spaces. Potential private-sector occupants in such spaces could offer the schools in which they would be located a good deal. They could provide pro bono expertise in areas such as technology and business operations in exchange for an arrangement to provide reduced or in some cases free rent. And perhaps more important, they could provide mentorship for students and/or teachers, paid internships at the high school level, assistance with college and career counseling, and other needed supports. And while schools are very busy during school hours, many school buildings are unoccupied in late afternoons and evenings, and on weekends, times when access to such spaces for private-sector occupants would be quite desirable. Many cities are on the lookout for spaces to use for business growth, with a variety of public funding, largely from economic development coffers. Some call this space business incubator space. But leveraging such space in schools is a way to allow those funds to be spent more creatively as incentives that would be of benefit to schools and students and directly to communities. Of course, closer connections to private businesses and entrepreneurs would have other benefits, including potential financial contributions to both schools, teachers, and parent associations.

Putting this into place would be a challenge, but is hardly impossible. Vacant school space could, via action by local school boards, be made available to existing local, regional, or state economic development agencies or local community development corporations, who in turn would market the space, ensure that occupants met key criteria for eligibility (i.e., providing paid internships, mentors for students and teachers, and so on), make any payments to the schools or districts for use of the space, and monitor key performance metrics and outcomes for the program.

This can be embarked upon district by district or state by state. In addition to the benefits to schools and students, this would have direct benefits to entrepreneurs, and especially start-ups. Moreover, gaining engagement with the private sector in this way will also expand the support systems that education systems very much need by getting private-sector leaders engaged in the real issues facing our schools.

Of course, the use of such space need not be provided only to for-profit businesses. Not-for-profit social service providers or arts and culture organizations might also be woven into such a plan. They, too, in exchange for favorable rent and access to unique facilities, might provide needed support services directly to students in the form of social services or the arts.

Education Operations Brought into the Twenty-First Century

America's K–12 education system has always resisted federal top-down leadership. Of course there have been federal initiatives that have been not only valuable but in certain cases essential. The federal government got involved in issues of discrimination on the basis of race, gender, and the ability to serve students with special needs because states and local school districts quite simply failed in their responsibility to meet the needs of all students in an equitable fashion. This led to federal law, federal regulation, and federal funding decisions. The same is also true of the role of states or the courts. They too have been forced to intervene when local districts allocated funding in a less than equal fashion, in order to protect the rights of all students.

However, notwithstanding the instances where federal and state education leadership, often urged to do so by political leaders, have acted, in the main educational decisions are made and will continue to be made at the local level. For a host of reasons this makes eminent good sense. States and the federal government ought not dictate who should be chosen to be an assistant principal, a principal, or a district superintendent, assuming they meet established criteria for performance.

They ought not be involved in school openings or school closures and how funding is appropriated to local schools under their jurisdiction. Making decisions close to the action is wise and in fact essential. However, in addition to being engaged in education, teaching, and learning, local school districts are also involved in a range of what can be characterized as business operations. They order supplies, manage data centers, route school buses, manage a range of labor issues, including health and retirement plans, and are responsible for financial management of school and district budgets. Hardly any of these management and operation decisions are about pedagogy or local control. And perhaps most importantly, having those decisions and operations made at the local level makes them extremely duplicative and expensive. Financial inefficiency is important in this domain because funds spent at rates higher than they need to be on these management and operations issues deprive teachers and classrooms of the resources they need to do what education systems are supposed to do, which is first and foremost to educate America's children.

This is not simply an outsourcing opportunity. The example in this book of the private-sector role in the creation of Social Security is a good model. While put into place by a private company, the system was implemented as a genuine public-private partnership. In the operations of school systems, the same could take place, where a true public-private partnership focused on reducing unnecessary operating costs and then putting the savings into improved classroom services could be part of a joint incentive, with clear and measurable results.

New York State provides one example. There are 700 local school districts across the state. Some are very large. New York City, for example, is the largest school district in the nation; it serves more than a third of the over 3 million students in the state. There are other large districts as well, called the "Big Five," consisting of Buffalo, Rochester, Syracuse, Yonkers, and Utica, which represent another significant proportion of the state's student population. Taken together, the City of New York and the Big Five represent two-thirds of the students in the state, with the rest of the student population divided among a range of communities from the Canadian border to Long Island, some of which oversee education for only a few thousand students or less. The inefficiencies and increased costs of having each district manage all of their managerial and operations functions, like separate slices of a pie, performed in a very duplicative fashion, wind up costing the state and the localities significant amounts of money and sadly divert a substantial amount of resources away from classroom instruction, teaching, and important education and support services.

If any company acquired another company with separate purchasing, finance, data management, and human resources functions for every geography where the company did business, their first step would be to consolidate those functions, centralize them, achieve significant cost savings, and then dedicate the savings toward the business's core objectives.

This is where a unique public-private partnership could really help. Across the nation we spend nearly $600 billion annually on K–12 public education, and we spend on average $11,000 per pupil. Of that spending over 90 percent goes for instructional and support services, with the remaining 10 percent, roughly $60 billion, going toward administrative, operations, and managerial needs. Given the fact that this is all currently performed in a decentralized fashion with no focus on shared services, public education, were it to act in a more effective structured way, could achieve at least a 10 percent reduction. Thus, a potential savings of $6 billion could be realized with a different model for providing administrative, operational, and managerial services. That is a huge opportunity. Were $6 billion in new funding to be achieved in this way, and available for America's schools to spend, it could make a massive difference in things vitally important to student achievement. The resources could raise teacher and principal pay, reduce class size, add guidance and support services, or provide a combination of them all.

Achieving the target of $6 billion in savings to be distributed into enhanced classroom services and teacher compensation is the goal, but getting there and focusing and targeting these resources currently spent differently can only be done via a unique public-private partnership implemented state by state and district by district. Implementing an effort directed at freeing these resources and then reallocating them into classrooms would be achieved as follows:

A new national public-private not-for-profit entity would need to be created. It would assess the range of for-profit companies with expertise in assisting states and districts in the centralization of their operating and managerial costs across each state. It would offer a coalition of these firms an opportunity to be engaged in a range of services to a state's districts via a consolidated contract. The cost of those services would be provided to the state at a 20 percent discount, with another 30 percent of the cost absorbed by the companies, which in turn would receive a tax deduction for that portion of the operating cost as a contribution. The remaining 50 percent of the cost would be contributed equally by the state and its local school districts. And under this scenario 100 percent of the savings would accrue to the local districts and their schools. For a district it means paying 25 cents on the dollar with a return on their investment of $1 for every 25 cents they contributed to this effort. The resulting massive infusion to states, local districts, and individual schools would be tracked through an independent audit that would assess the cost savings versus the total value of resources reallocated, along with the effect on student achievement. This commonsense solution would require federal and state legislative and regulatory actions. But it would be implemented locally.

It would also require the establishment of a new not-for-profit entity or entities that would operate this program in partnership with states and localities, with the operating costs of that entity paid for by philanthropic contributions from major private and corporate foundations, enhanced by governmental contracts.

Reinforcing the Importance of Education

The above three initiatives need to be bolstered by all employers in the private sector in other meaningful and concrete ways to demonstrate their support for education improvement and do so in a very visible fashion. Currently, virtually all employers who interview a proposed candidate for a job ask to see evidence of a degree or certification, and sometimes they ask to see a transcript of academic achievement. However, most high school students seeking a summer job or a part-time job will never be asked for evidence of their academic achievement or be asked to produce evidence of success. This needs to change. A job should not be seen as being separate from education success, but connected to it. It would make a definitive change were all employers to ask their summer or part-time employees, while still in high school, to show them their last report card, and initiate a conversation about the importance of academic achievement, thus reinforcing the need for high levels of academic performance. Were this reform to be embraced, the message would be clear: academic achievement matters. In addition, for employees who have children in school, their employer ought to, as a matter of policy and practice, provide time off to attend parent-teacher conferences. This is routine for some large employers, though not all, but rare for employees who work for small or midsized businesses. We have seen actions on the state and local level to raise the minimum wage and provide paid sick leave, but time off to attend parent-teacher conferences is just as critical and sends an unequivocal message that parental involvement is connected to education success is not just important but essential.

The Education Solution

These innovative efforts, were they embraced, could be implemented immediately. They don't require an act of Congress or a massive financial investment on the part of business or government. They would address the challenge of the teacher shortage or skills crisis, now and into the future, with exemplary new teachers coming into our school systems in larger numbers, quickly, and in an affordable fashion via highly skilled professionals interested in an encore career.

They would also bring the operations and management of our school systems into the twenty-first century, with massive efficiencies and cost savings, freeing up billions of dollars in existing state and local funding that could put substantial new funding directly into the classroom, resulting in higher teacher salaries, reduced class sizes, the provision of increased guidance and support services, and, most important, resulting in improved student achievement. We would see a deeper connection between education and economic development via the creation of education makerspaces in schools across cities and states nationwide, stimulating engagement with the private and not-for-profit sector to make other investments in our children's future. This can be perhaps even more significant than the collaboration that created Social Security in the 1930s. Finally, were all employers to reinforce the importance of education by asking to see report cards, and offering employees with school-aged children time off to attend parent-teacher conferences, the importance of education will be reinforced along with the need to support the work of educators.

Concurrent with the specifics I have outlined, we need a renewed consensus about the overall need for improving our education system. We need to discard the practice of what can be characterized as the "blame game." Lack of progress in education is not the fault of just some, it's the result of action, or inaction, by all of us. We need a focus on innovation in the classroom and in all support systems, a focus on quality teaching and how to support it, on enhanced standards and accountability, on moving beyond the needless controversy over the Common Core or school choice, and the need to have higher standards and higher results, and on the connection between school, college, and career so we can see more students prepared for the opportunities of today and tomorrow. Movement in this direction will require a commitment to end petty divisions and instead build consensus behind what we can all do together to create opportunity for today's students and tomorrow's. The message to parents also needs to be clear. Higher standards are how we raise the bar for achievement, and this effort needs their full support and an understanding that higher standards, higher achievement, and more effective accountability will lead to increased economic opportunity for America's youth.

Leadership by the private sector in support of education is not an option. It is essential.

Economic Development and Jobs

Unlike in the area of education, the majority of U.S. spending on job training is not spent by government; it is spent by the private sector, not the public sector. An Urban Institute study released more than a dozen years ago, but still largely accurate, put spending on job training by the private sector at between 9 and 12 times greater than all federal and state spending on job training combined. Private business job training spending in the early years of the twenty-first century was pegged by the Urban Institute at about $50 billion a year, with federal spending at about $5 billion, and state spending across the 50 states at about $600 million. While most of the effective ways to innovate in the area of job creation and workforce improvements are left to employers, the role of the federal government in particular and states as well can be significant.

The major federal programs have been reshaped and renamed over the last half century. They started with the Manpower Development and Training Act in the 1960s, renamed the Comprehensive Employment and Training Act of the 1970s, the Job Training Partnership Act of the 1980s, the Workforce Investment Act of the 1990s, and currently the Workforce Innovation and Opportunities Act. But while the names have changed, and the levels of spending have fluctuated, the overall success of the programs has varied. One thing has been consistent: most independent analysts have called for a greater level of public-private partnership, more local control, a focus on those most in need, and jobs with the highest level of pay and growth opportunity. In spite of some successes, it would be hard to argue with the fact that much more needs to be done, and the focus cannot only be on the unemployed, but just as importantly those currently employed but at risk of their employment ending. And while job training is important, it must go hand in glove with education. Both need to focus on jobs with the best opportunity and stability, addressing the variety of needs of individual populations. And most important, like any enterprise, they ought to be up to date, using the most effective and innovative approaches, in the most effective ways.

According to a recent Pew Research Center survey conducted with the help of the Markel Foundation, fairly dramatic changes are taking place in America's workplace. They are affecting America's economy in significant ways, but as we look forward into the future the effects may be even more dramatic. Let's start with the facts. The number of workers in occupations requiring average and above-average education and training grew markedly, from 49 million in 1980 to 83 million in 2015. In that 35-year period it was a dramatic 70 percent increase. Couple this with the fact that a very extensive survey completed by Pew showed that more than half of Americans in the workforce, 54 percent, said it is "essential" for them to get additional training and improved skills just to keep up with changing job requirements.

Given the pace of change in the global economy these figures are more than a current crisis. They are a clear demonstration that this threat to our economy will only increase. Jobs with the highest growth rates and those with the highest compensation require higher skill levels, both technical and interpersonal. According to the Pew study, more than 6 in 10 people, or 63 percent, of adults working with a bachelor's degree say they believe they will need to advance their workplace skills in order to keep their jobs. Among the skills identified are some of the workplace skills IBM focused on in the creation of P-TECH for entry-level jobs. But looking at those currently in the workplace, 85 percent say they will need to improve their writing and problem-solving skills, and roughly 7 in 10 say they will need to improve their math and science skills. A third of respondents say they don't have the education and training to get ahead in their current jobs. When Americans are asked who is responsible for addressing this challenge, they point fingers in all directions: at workers themselves, at the education and higher education systems, at government at all levels, and at employers. The reality is that a potential solution cannot be laid at the feet of any one segment; it requires action, collaboration, and shared investment from all sectors.

What the Pew study tells us is clear: we are facing a crisis in skills not only for those entering the workforce, but also for those who are currently in it. If we don't find a way to build education and skill levels of those in the workforce now, the risk is they will be moved toward retirement without sufficient resources to sustain them, or, worse, drop out of the workforce altogether. If significant numbers of workers are not given an opportunity to improve their skills, the economic cost will be significant, and the cost and risk to society and to all Americans would be just as significant, perhaps even more so. If we believe that income inequality is a problem now, the likelihood is that disparities will increase exponentially if we focus only on the economic threat of other countries or of immigrants. The problem is ours to solve, and this significant economic risk could, wthout action, threaten millions of jobs.

A Commitment to Stabilizing and Improving the Skills of the Workforce

Retraining and increasing the skills and abilities of the existing workforce will not be easy, but it is definitely doable. We could start with the use of data analytics to review the skills match, job area by job area, industry by industry, and geography by geography to determine what types of skills and education are needed to keep the largest number of people currently in the workforce successfully employed. Likely this would focus on a combination of workplace skills and specific, or hard, skills, especially those connected to technology expertise. Some of the ways in which this skill building and enhancement would be delivered would involve online learning developed by educational institutions in partnership with affected businesses. But other elements would be delivered in more traditional ways, supported and enhanced by mentors and guidance staff who would reinforce the provision of additional training and education. The delivery system for providing these education and skills to the targeted population would include existing educational institutions that would have incentives to offer the courses and credentials matched to individual needs, working hand in glove with employers.

A cost-sharing model involving institutions and individuals would be essential to make these efforts affordable. Individuals would have to engage in these activities and do so on their own time, while businesses that would be the beneficiaries of the enhanced skills of their employees would also share in the cost, as would government at the local, state, and national levels. It should be clear that keeping more people employed would have a significant return on investment. If the combined funding available for this challenge is close to $60 billion, how to deliver it in an effective fashion needs to be determined and then acted upon with respect to who assumes the cost. As a matter of principle and practice, it ought to be shared between the individuals affected, their employers, and government at the local, state, and national levels. Each actor is affected by the results and must have "skin in the game." But who pays, and how much they pay, is only part of the answer to the problem. The second component is who provides the solution, what the solution looks like, and, perhaps most important, what would an accountability system look like that would help ensure that a solution that is affordable is also scalable, sustainable, and effective. If individuals whose current employment is in jeopardy are given upgraded skills and stay successfully employed and productive for a fixed period of time, the financial investment made by all parties would be recouped or exceeded. A routine independent assessment of the degree to which objectives were met could ensure continued success.

This can best be achieved in a block grant approach, where businesses might outline a specific number of jobs that are at risk and offer to provide a matching grant covering the education and training costs, along with their at-risk employees offering to assume shared responsibility for enhancing skills and education on their own time. How these resources would be split, whether 90 percent private and 10 percent public or another ratio, needs to be determined and agreed to. On-the-job training, education, online courses, mentoring, and other program components should not be overregulated, and success would be judged based on the number and kind of jobs saved, the salaries provided, and over what period of time.

The core element of the challenge would be to effectively utilize and combine effective online education and course offerings that would focus on needed workplace skills and specific hard skills, implemented in conjunction with on-the-job training combined with actual training courses, needed coaching, and mentorship. Credentials based on specific program and outcome measures would be rewarded. Overall cost can vary based on individual needs, but there would have to be metrics for

success developed jointly by the employers and government and vali-
dated by the other partners and collaborators.

However, once put in place this could have a significant stabilizing
effect on jobs and the economy.

Apprenticeships 2.0

Apprenticeships have historically been a very well-regarded component of
the transition to employment, and not just in the United States. The model
of apprenticeships, begun in the Middle Ages and further developed and
implemented across multiple geographies over hundreds of years, has been
critical to providing the education and skills training needed to effectively
make a transition into the workforce. Its birth and development resulted
from leadership in the employer community where jobs and careers existed.
While initially involving young people between the ages of 10 and 15, and
also involving live-in arrangements, preparing young people for a host
of skilled labor, apprenticeship has matured to involve on-the-job training and study across an expanded number of job categories. In Germany,
often cited as a model in the implementation of successful apprenticeship
programs, 342 trades are successfully served by the national apprenticeship
program across job categories and industries. Investments in such programs
are critical and connected to economic growth and stability.

In the United States, we currently significantly underinvest in apprenticeship grants, with only about $200 million annually provided by the
U.S. Labor Department to support the needed education and training
designed to help those who are unemployed or underemployed obtain the
skills needed to have a more productive future. Given that overall spending
on job training between government and private sources is in the neighborhood of $60 billion, the amount of money we spend on apprentice-
ships is incredibly small. This amount of money is woefully inadequate, but
if all we did was spend more—and while we ought to do so—we might
make some improvements, but unless we married added spending with
doing so in a significantly smarter fashion, nothing close to what is needed
would take place. In 2008 in the midst of the recession, 50,000 Americans
completed apprenticeships; in 2016, the number declined to about 48,000.

In one large state, New York, the number was a little over 5,000
participants statewide. The actual number of participants who successfully

completed their program in 2016 in New York State was only 945, in Florida it was a bit over 1,000, and in Pennsylvania it was 1,100. In a small state like Maine only 27 residents completed an apprenticeship program in 2016. The number of active apprenticeship programs across all 50 states declined as well, from about 23,000 programs to 22,000 today. Perhaps most disturbing, the programs are not focused on the areas of economic growth in the way that they ought to, with only 982 participants in apprenticeships focused on the information technology industry and fewer than 300 participating in professional, scientific, and technical services. The contrast with skilled immigrants is startling. In New York State there are over 93,560 H-1B visa–certified positions, with an average salary of $82,000 a year.

Given the jobs and wage crisis facing the nation, it is clear that the apprenticeship program plays a marginal role at best in meeting the challenge of preparing large numbers of unemployed or underemployed Americans with the education and skills needed to earn a living wage and have a respectable chance for at least a middle-class lifestyle.

Apprenticeship 2.0, if implemented, could significantly expand the number of Americans undertaking an apprenticeship and not just increase the numbers but focus them on high-wage and high-growth job areas. It could make sure the jobs trained for connect to labor market data about where the most and best job opportunities exist, give employers a more significant role in determining what level of education and training is needed to provide a stable and effective transition into the workforce, and ensure that the funding appropriated for apprenticeships is connected to solid outcomes and successes as opposed to simply the number of participants served.

Step one would be to turn apprenticeship program funds into a block grant as well. It would still be a competitive grant program, but the competition would be connected to a highly regarded credential or certification, and would be effectuated at the state level, with deep collaboration between employers and the government. Shared funding would permit the employer, in partnership, not solely the government, to determine how the funding would be allocated between education, on-the-job training, and incentives for completion, and would be based on accountability with metrics for performance. And a portion of the funding would reward an increase in not only the number of people who complete their apprenticeship, but also the number of successful apprenticeship completions from the most vulnerable populations. The goal would be to increase the total funding appropriation from $200 million to $500 million and to increase the number of those successfully completing apprenticeships from 48,000 to 150,000. It would also provide a focus on current jobs that are threatened by the need for further training and education. By stripping out overregulation and needless bureaucracy, providing incentives for success, and tying the program more heavily toward where the jobs are now and are likely to be in the future, it would provide funding for a program that would be more significant to the economy.

Many of the existing apprenticeship programs are of high quality. In New York State, for example, the largest programs are for skilled labor such as electricians, skilled construction, sheet metal workers, plumbers, machinists, and tool and die makers. All to the good and very important and necessary. But few are in occupations in information technology, health care, and advanced manufacturing. This will require innovation and additional focus.

To put this into place, leaders from the private sector would need to make this effort a top priority and exercise leadership, working with governmental leadership in collaboration at both the state and local levels. They could identify the ways in which technology, especially involving online training and education, could be designed and then offered across industries. They could provide training and education opportunities not only to meet their own needs but also those of their supply chains and vendors. This would also require the engagement of the education sector, especially community and technical colleges, in partnership with employers, offering more opportunities for the private sector to provide not just jobs but as adjunct faculty and partners in course designs. There could also be shared financial incentives and rewards for things connected to the success of this type of effort, including promotions, mentorships, and compensation levels.

Importantly, if success in the workplace involves the need for social or health services, the provision of such services, either by the employer or by not-for-profit organizations with this expertise, would be permitted and recognized as a needed and legitimate expense, and built into the apprenticeship program design. Right now, there is no recognition of the need for such services or the importance of their integration into an apprenticeship program. This has the negative effect of making the program ineffective for participants who need such services and reduces success rates for those who have a such an ummet need, if it is left unmet. The need could be met by an employer or a not-for-profit organization and the benefit would essentially pay for itself with improved success rates for those involved.

Based on expected success in expanding the number of successfully completed apprenticeships and their connection to job growth, we could easily see the investment in apprenticeships increasing significantly, with the results impacting economic development and employment stability and growth.

Jobs and Growth in the Twenty-First Century

Putting these kinds of jobs and education initiatives into place would directly affect the issue of economic growth, and in a very positive way. It would ease the threat to those in the workforce now by providing them with the enhanced education and skills to continue in the workforce, be more successful, and also ease the way in which skills and education could be provided to allow those currently unemployed or underemployed to successfully enter the workforce, thus protecting, enhancing, and providing new opportunities for large numbers of vulnerable workers, directly addressing the issue of income inequality. Moving forward in these ways would not simply be an investment in a new government grant program. It would facilitate the creation of an entirely new and deep public-private partnership designed to leverage existing resources in a new way, providing a shared solution to perhaps the most important problem facing society, jobs, and economic growth, that unless addressed threatens the nation's economic well-being.

This is not to say that existing government spending and private-sector initiatives don't work. Clearly some do, and some don't. But the initiatives outlined here stretch the envelope and would generate significant job growth and stabilize existing jobs by putting a critically important focus on both skills and education. Of course, it need not end with these initiatives either. The same type of innovation that the private sector uses to create and grow new businesses, or reinvent those that exist, can in close cooperation with both the public and volunteer sectors lead to ways of addressing other challenges that impact society, too.

A Brighter Future

As we move into the future, it is important that we make a clear and certain break with the past. Relying solely on government legislation and regulation to govern corporate behavior as the only way of penalizing negative behavior, while sometimes effective, is clearly not the only effective model for the future. The best models of effective corporate responsibility encourage excellence and raise the bar for those companies to substantially increase their commitments. They also inspire others to choose to model that behavior. However, if current and past actions teach us anything, relying solely on these models of excellence is not an effective future strategy in and of itself. There are things that can be done to move us forward in a different and more productive way.

The focus on ethics and community service embedded into all levels of education, and into the world of work, is step one. Nothing will change behavior more than building a culture of ethics and service into the very nature of what we do and how we do it. Second is inspiring the next generation of leaders to lead and to build the structures that will encourage and support those who do. Next will be efforts to engage in some significant pathbreaking changes resulting in concrete measurable ways not just to address problems, but to solve them. The suggestions of ways to address the teacher shortage and teacher skill crises are real, and a solution is within our control to enact. Making makerspace part of education produces benefits to schools and their students. The same is true of building cross-sector solutions to the education challenge and demonstrating what can be done with a commitment to determining innovative ways to proceed, as is the case with the skills crisis and the need to spur economic growth by improving the quality of those in the workforce and those hoping to enter it. Taken altogther, these initiatives are designed to address both education and economic development challenges, and while they have a modest, shared investment, these initiatives will demonstrate how we can produce measurable results, building interest and support to take these approaches to the next level.

But this need not be the end of what we do. Were we able to end the blame game and focus on true public-private partnership, combining our best resources in these effective ways, it would provide a structural model for the future.

There are many other societal issues that could be addressed in the same fashion if we have the will to do things differently.

But to do this we need to take down the barriers that far too often divide us, such as those between economic sectors, and create the necessary incentives for cross-sector collaboration and promote such a change in behavior as the ticket to success. Standing on the sidelines and hurling criticism at one another is simply a tactic, not a solution; understanding what drives us apart and what can bring us together, and then acting with common goals and objectives in ways that benefit both business and society, is how we will determine our future success. From risk to reward.

Conclusion

The compelling challenge for business and society today is to address cross-sector corporate citizenship in an innovative, meaningful, and effective way, transitioning from risk to reward. What do I mean by risk? Well, there is a significant risk facing the private sector if it continues to be viewed in an entirely negative way. That risk is considerable. While views may fluctuate with respect to the public's view of business or government, a decidedly negative view of business will, if it continues, lead to a range of actions in the near term that could have any number of negative results. If the past is prologue to the future, such negatives views will inhibit innovation, creativity, and job growth, and impede positive economic development. Put simply, there is a significant cost in doing nothing. There is also an escalating risk to business if it invites continued criticism resulting from some bad actors that engage in unethical and unacceptable behavior even while others function in a positive way. Businesses that behave poorly and don't treat their corporate responsibility seriously face the risk of alienating their customers,

171

their shareholders, and their employees. Their corporate life span will be short and largely unsuccessful. Those that function positively may run the risk of being tarred with the same brush used on those that behave badly.

Bad business behavior also risks negative reactions, and rightly so, from the media and the public. Yet this often leads to both governmental legislation and regulation that can inhibit growth of all business or damage the value of some brands. There is even a risk to companies that are exemplary leaders in corporate responsibility should others in their industry or in the private sector as a whole behave badly. History and current events provide a clear and compelling narrative that a failure to understand the important and positive role that business can play in society carries a significant risk. Businesses that behave poorly will and should face consequences, but so does the entire private sector.

Risk goes far beyond the private sector. A uniformly negative view of business and its role in society creates a risk to all sectors. Apart from the facts not justifying that view, harsh and negative views of business make the private sector less likely to energize its businesses and employees in positive and innovative ways, making them less likely to publicly display their leadership in corporate responsibility and on societal issues overall and instead be wary of any and all behavior that could lead to further exposure and potential risk. The value of business leadership on a host of issues is significant, and causing it to retreat is not a desirable outcome for anyone.

But there is another side to the coin. It is about turning risk into reward, and realizing real sustained value. And there is a significant reward to both business and society if corporate responsibility is treated with an importance equal to executing effective business strategy and achieving economic success. It is not separate but in fact integral to businesses' and society's economic success. Businesses that have strong principles and values undergirded with a deep appreciation of the link between ethical conduct and business success, and display their leadership in the way they conduct themselves and inspire others, are in fact more economically successful companies. They attract and retain better talent, and they have fewer risks to their reputation, their brand, and their bottom line. Those that work in partnership with government and civil society to address societal problems in an effective way can take their business performance to even higher levels by building community stability. Such companies have seen a very concrete and tangible return on their investments. They see concrete results that are linked directly to their bottom line. They are more competitive and position themselves in a way that gives them the permission they need to operate. The phrase "doing well by doing good" is not just a phrase; it is a reality documented by fact.

There are concrete actions that businesses can take not only to achieve financial success, but also to maximize those rewards. They can and should act in those ways. But they can do more. They can achieve new performance levels, maximizing those rewards, but only if business, government, and civil society cease operating singly and instead work together. America has a number of serious problems, many of which are outlined in this book. Yet we are also a resource-rich nation. We have massive resources in the private, public, and civil society sectors. We have a love of innovation and an entrepreneurial spirit that supports economic growth and opportunity. We also have a history and commitment to sharing our strengths and resources with those who are less fortunate. If we combine our resources—financial, technological, entrepreneurial, and practical—in effective ways, we may not solve every social problem that exists today, but we can and will make significant progress, and we can track that progress in demonstrable ways. A cleaner and more stable environment is not impossible, a better-functioning education system is achievable as well, and a more effective social safety net and a safer and more humane society are within our grasp, all of which will produce quantifiable economic returns for all Americans, at all economic levels.

We can get there by learning the lessons of history along with our day-to-day experiences in the present. But most important, we can determine what we can do differently, realizing a more positive future by going from risk to reward. Does business success have any lessons we can take forward? Absolutely.

True business success relies on a range of assumptions and activities all operating in concert with one another. It starts with a compelling, often innovative business idea. The idea is fueled by a combination of financial resources and talent that together turn that idea into an achievable business plan and strategy. That strategy then needs metrics to assess levels of success, adaptations that will build upon success, a consensus about the tasks needed to maximize success, and a strategy to communicate and market that success in both the short and the long term. It also needs a recognition of the barriers that may impede that success, including an understanding of the competition and the will and means to eliminate those barriers. A failure to understand the importance and challenge to business and society of going from risk to reward will impede both business success and societal gains. A full appreciation and application of the lessons of business success applied as an effective means of addressing the challenges of business and society provides us with a framework and road map for realizing that success.

When IBM had its one hundredth anniversary and celebrated the history of the company, it focused on two core lessons for success and longevity. They are useful for all to remember. First was a commitment to change. Circumstances change all the time, and when they do, or even better in anticipation of when they do, successful enterprises embrace the need to change, and effectively put their change strategies into place. Were IBM a company that still only made typewriters or time clocks, could it have sustained itself? Likely not. In the twenty-first century, the pace of change has accelerated, and the need to embrace it has become even more of a necessity than ever before. Successful businesses learn and practice this all the time. American Express moved into new businesses, as did IBM. Newer and younger businesses are learning to reinvent themselves at a rapid pace. The second lesson for success and longevity in sustaining a business is what ought never change, and that is a commitment to ethics, core values, and principles. Success linked to ethical practices is essential, as is an appreciation and understanding of why trust and personal responsibility are critically important factors. Many successful businesses embrace this view.

Governmental success is also connected to the same two important lessons. Governments at all levels must embrace change as well. It wasn't until the end of the Second World War that we adapted our public education systems to make high school mandatory. It fueled economic growth in the second half of the twentieth century. If we still had a K–8 mandatory education system and high school was optional, we would not be a great nation. In the mid-1930s, Social Security created a secure future for Americans at retirement age; that was a big change and it sustained itself for decades. When Americans returned from the Second World War, an innovative effort called the GI Bill was implemented. It was new and it provided opportunities different from how veterans were given opportunities after prior wars. And still, the lesson of what not to change—principles and ethics—also applies to the public sector. As a nation we still embrace the principles our Founding Fathers embodied in the Constitution and Bill of Rights. And we take pride in the legacy of both documents and their ability to sustain our democracy and a free society.

The core lessons of excellence and longevity, what to change and what not to, apply directly to corporate responsibility as well.

The first lesson we need to embrace and anticipate is the need for change in the basic way in which we understand corporate responsibility. Corporate responsibility is not simply checkbook philanthropy or "giving back." A review of history and the present shows incredible examples of private-sector leadership involving transformative actions that provided large-scale benefit to society having nothing to do with simple cash donations. Such efforts affected labor practices, diversity, environmental actions, and community engagement. They did involve making financial commitments, both necessary and needed, but the benefits went beyond a tax deduction.

This is the perfect opportunity to reinforce and perhaps even reinvent the connection between business and society. Having a strong set of values and ethical principles is critically important to any well-functioning business, but those principles need to go beyond being communicated and understood. They need to be put into practice with the incentives and rewards behind them that will make them sustainable and scalable. Community service tied to business skills is one way that those ethical principles and core values can be put into practice, and this needs to be reinforced. Such programs benefit the individuals who perform community service, and provide equal added benefits to companies and society. These efforts ought not be separate from work but part of it, with all of the required elements and rewards built in, including promotions, recognition, and financial reward. Businesses can do this.

There are no real barriers to getting it done, but if it were prized by government, encouraged and supported by governmental actions through collaboration and incentives, and highlighted in the media, the practice would go beyond being embraced and practiced by only the best companies, or the largest ones. Media attention and societal encouragement of such practices would spur the actions on at higher and higher levels of performance and this work could help address critical societal problems, enhance skills and talent in the workplace, and generate a triple benefit. Environmental practices and a commitment to racial, ethnic, and gender diversity and inclusion should follow the same pathway. These efforts require encouragement and incentives along with collaboration and partnerships achieved via deep and close collaboration among all sectors.

I hope the examples of best practices outlined in this book demonstrate that innovation and long-term commitments demonstrate what can be achieved. These examples are demonstrations of success. But encouragement, reward, and support of such practices would make a huge difference. They would expand positive actions from some to many, and make those activities integral to business operations across the private sector. A deep commitment to corporate responsibility will result from it and be embraced and supported.

However, change is also critically important in a programmatic fashion allowing companies to apply to their corporate responsibility efforts the same tools they apply to all other aspects of their businesses. We need them to apply innovation, public-private partnership, and metrics that demonstrate actual results. This can be best accomplished if companies have incentives to contribute their most valuable assets, their talent and expertise, combined with their financial capabilities. And finally, change can also be a core element in how corporate responsibility is structured within companies, providing an integrated way to manage the core elements of corporate responsibility and elevating it within the corporate structure by providing access to corporate key decision makers at the absolute highest levels.

The corporate responsibility function within companies is structured and managed very differently across companies. In some cases, it is part of marketing, in other cases part of human resources or communications. In many companies the title of a key function oftentimes starts with the word "chief." The chief financial officer manages a company's finances, the chief operations officer is the day-to-day lead on all manner of operations, and the chief marketing officer or chief communications officer likewise head critical functions tied to the business strategy of the company. The same should be true of the individual and staff responsible for corporate responsibility. It should have the same stature and access to key decision makers that will help minimize risk and maximize reward. But by elevating its importance it also will make it easier to integrate all of the functions that intersect in an effective way. The corporate foundation model is widely used and is important too, but it cannot begin and end there. An integrated operational strategy that combines all core elements of corporate responsibility with the requisite stature is essential to manage this work effectively, and, most important, deliver a concrete return on investment to the company and its shareholders.

The second change needed in corporate responsibility is that core values need to be embraced and understood but then put into practice and reinforced in the same ways that all other exemplary business practices are practiced. Employee volunteerism is important and needs to be encouraged and supported. It will build loyalty in the workforce and support in the community. Engagement with civil society is also vitally important. Service on not-for-profit boards, participation on school boards and community boards, service on parent-teacher associations—this needs to be encouraged and supported by the private sector, in very real ways. Citizenship is important and is connected to ethics and values. It needs to be understood as something that will build and enhance skills and develop community stability and engagement, and is part of business success and not separate from it. Creating specific goals in these areas, metrics to determine success against those goals and how to proceed in the future, is not only possible but essential.

Beyond just business and the private sector, we need to elevate and embrace the commitment to ethics and values that have been at the core of our nation since it came into being. Truth, justice, and the American way are not just three words; they define what this nation stands for. Of course, without strict interpretation of every word or syllable in the nation's founding documents, it is clear that the nation was founded on high principles that included a strong set of values and ethics. We can argue about whether those values and ethics as they were written were truly meant to apply to all and not to some, but hopefully we can all now agree that they should be applied to all. The private sector can do a good deal here, by raising the level of importance ethics and values play in their economic success and business strategy, integrating them into all they do, and making a commitment to diversity at all levels. But here again this cannot be the responsibility of business alone. Government, education leaders, civil society, and all Americans need to reinforce, encourage, and reward such behavior in concrete and measurable ways and augment it by putting into place actions that integrate ethics and values into education and American life. All K–12 and higher education institutions ought to embed ethics and community service into a sound education program.

Social media allows everyone to know in an instant about bad behavior, but, sadly, instead of limiting or eliminating such behavior, it may wind up doing just the opposite, encouraging others to model that negative behavior and replicate it. We need to consciously and effectively make sure that we are focusing even more attention on the practices we most admire and want to encourage and elevating them and integrating them into the core elements of business and governmental practice.

The genesis for this book is based on my career in leadership roles in the private, public, and not-for-profit sectors. While the idea for it started during the 2016 presidential campaign, it has its genesis much earlier than that. It was not one candidate or one elected or appointed official who chose to point a finger at the private sector for its responsibility for virtually all of America's societal problems, and it did not come from officials or the media representing any one particular political persuasion either. It was pervasive. And it has its genesis in the past. It is my hope that this book will have set the record straight and demonstrated that facts are more relevant than name calling or opinion. The real purpose of the book was to go beyond that and identify and outline, via fact-based examples and potential opportunities, those specific and concrete steps that can and should be taken to mobilize all sectors to work together in ways that will make a significant impact on societal problems while at the same time enhance business success with real and quantifiable economic returns for us all.

There is in fact another path forward. There always is. It is time to get beyond negative talk and the status quo, and instead chart a different course. We can do this, and the time is now. It will begin with a fact-based understanding of the role business has played and currently plays in society, both positively and negatively. It will debunk the myth that every problem can be easily laid at the doorstep of the private sector or any sector for that matter. But that is not the end of the challenge; it is more like the beginning. It also requires an understanding of how government, civil society, and business can work together in new, different, and effective ways to combine their resources, and positively impact society and create economic benefit for us all. We need to embrace some of what I would hope are the creative, yet achievable, ideas outlined in this book, and not simply nod our heads and say they are interesting. We must move forward and implement them.

And, not stopping there, but working in collaborative ways, we must come up with new ideas and implement them as well. We must change, and embrace that change. Business needs to embrace the lessons laid out here, but it cannot do this alone.

We must have a common understanding and a shared vision of the future and then move forward together to realize all that we can do together to make the benefit of corporate responsibility real. We must go from risk to reward.

About the Author

Stan Litow has had a lengthy high-level career in business, government, education, and civil society. Serving under three CEOs, he led IBM's corporate citizenship programs and the IBM Foundation for nearly 25 years, where he created some of the world's most innovative corporate social responsibility efforts, including P-TECH, World Community Grid, and the Corporate Service Corps. At IBM he organized and helped lead three National Education Summits for the U.S. president, the nation's governors, CEOs, and education leaders. Before his IBM career he served as deputy chancellor of schools for the City of New York, the nation's largest school system, where he pioneered significant education reforms. He also founded and led a major think tank, Interface, that helped the City of New York cope with its last fiscal crisis. Prior to that he served under the mayor of New York City as executive director of the New York City Urban Corps, the nation's largest college intern program, and served on a range of advisory panels for the president of the United States and the governor of New York, where he chairs its Academic Affairs Committee. He is a global thought leader on critical policy issues including education, jobs, and the economy.

Stan lives in New York City with his life partner, Amy Brenna.

Index